Dreamlike Recording of East Capital

YuanLao Meng(Song Dynasty)

Translated by Bin Liu & Jirong Liu

A panoramic description of a capital with 1.5 millions about 1200 years ago by a writer at that time

While every precaution has been taken in the preparation of this book, the publisher assumes no responsibility for errors or omissions, or for damages resulting from the use of the information contained herein.

DREAMLIKE RECORDING OF EAST CAPITAL

First edition. January 4, 2024.

Copyright © 2024 Yuanlao Meng.

ISBN: 979-8224953066

Written by Yuanlao Meng.

Preface

I followed my father who was an official all over the country, in 1103 we came to East Capital. We lived in a house at the south side of a small alley west of Gold Beam Bridge. I grew up in the capital. As people lived in the capital with large population and plentiful material things for a long peaceful time, young children only learned how to beat a drum and dance, adults with gray hairs did not know any fighting weaponry. One festival came after another all year around, in every festival there would be a main theme: In Glutinous Rice Flour Dumpling Festival to watch lanterns in January, in Mid-Autumn Festival to watch moon in August, in Major Snow to watch snow in November, in February to watch booming flowers, in July Seventh to pray for bestowing skill and intellect, in September Ninth to climb hills and appreciate chrysanthemum, to watch the navy to practise in the lake, to play and appreciate flowers in royal gardens. When I raised my head, I would see varnished buildings, painted pavilions and hotels, engraved and painted doors, and curtains adorned with pearls. Carved and festooned carriages parked along streets, precious and rare horses were running in streets. Ornaments of gold and jewelry would dazzle my eyes, smells of perfumes were emanating from soft silk clothes and embroidered waist band. When I passed by whorehouse, I could hear new songs just developed and see beautiful smiling faces; in tea house people were playing bamboo pipe and plucking stringed instrument. Goods from other places were sent to and sold in the city, people from all over other places were doing businesses in the city. The treasures and rare articles from other places were sold in markets; dishes of various tastes and styles were prepared in the kitchens of restaurants. Flowers were set at the sides of streets, thus people could watch flowers without spring outing; sounds of vertical bamboo flute and drum were floating to sky from families holding banquets. Exquisite workmanship made me feel I was in a new world, extravagant style made me feel exhilarated and inspired. If I wanted to see the emperor, I could see him in Lantern Festival when he was watching lanterns in Declare Kindness Building(Xuan De Lou) or when he was visiting Gold Bright Lake(Jin Ming Chi). Of course I could wait on his way to go to south suburb to pray to Heaven and worship his ancestors. I could frequently watch the wedding procession for princesses and princes. There was a grand hall constructed for royal meeting, promulgation of new decrees, selection of candidates for officials etc. There was a smelting and casting plant which could produce cauldrons and big cauldrons etc. in a very short time. If one wanted to see the registered prostitutes and musicians, one could see them on their way back at the end of the banquets held in government offices or royal palace. If one wanted to see the sudden change of a man's lot, one could watch the new candidates who had already passed the imperial examination were summoned to pay respects to the emperor or the new candidate who was appointed as an official based on his ability and royal interview. I had spent dozens years in the capital for having fun, watching various scenes without being fed up a bit.

Suddenly the Khitan army came to the capital, I left the city in 1128 one year after the invasion, came to the south to flee from the war, wandered in different places, felt lonely and entered a stage of my life like setting glow. I could not help but think about the past, the beautiful scenery and things and the customs and the peaceful living, at the moment they only became melancholy regrets to me. Recently when I met with my relatives, we talked about the past, the young people who did not live and experience in the city could only imagine what the city was like, I worried if such a kind of status prolongs for a long time, people could not get a true picture about the people, things and custom, that would be a great regret. Thus I recalled the people, places and things carefully, put them in a proper order and time sequence in this book, I hoped when readers opened this book, they would see and witness the grand occasions of the past. In past an ancient man once visited the legendary fairyland, he enjoyed what he saw very much. At the moment I am recalling the past, I have a melancholy feeling, don't I wake up from the dream of the legendary fairyland too? Thus I call the book *Dreamlike Recording*. But the capital was huge with so many places, people and things, and for some places I did not experience by myself but just was told by other people, therefore definitely something would miss in my accounting. It would be a great honor to have some old and educated respectable men coming from the capital to supplement and edit the book to make it more complete. The words used in this book are mundane folk language, I don't try to use more refined words as I want ordinary people to be able to read this book, I hope you can understand my real intention when you read this book.

New Year's Eve in ShaoXing at January 22, 1148 AD by YuanLao Meng

Notes from Translators

Song Dynasty is divided into two periods. What this book describes is related to North Song(960-1127 AD). Due to policy of the founding ancestor, North Song did very well in economy but not very good in defense. Though it owned plenty of wealth, it had been bullied constantly by two nations at the north and northwest side of the country. In 1127 Khitan army invaded the capital, took the capital, then came to the end of North Song Dynasty.

Another son of Emperor Hui (Who was captured by Khitan army with his son—a new emperor got the throne from his father just one year before the occupation) flew to south with his ministers, established South Song Dynasty (1127-1279 AD) in a place at current Hangzhou City. South Dynasty held the smallest territory among the united dynasties of China.

The identity of the author of the book, YuanLao Meng, is still a mystery as except this book, he left nothing else. None mentioned his name around the period and later time except about the book. There were many guesses about his identity, but none was sure which guess is right. Some of people think he might have used a pen name and be a descendant of royal family.

The book described the lively scenes and customs etc. about East Capital with a population of 1.5 millions around 1120 AD. East Capital is located at current Kaifeng City. Kaifeng City has only about 5.25 millions people at the moment. There is a painting called *East Capital in Tomb Sweeping Day,* which painted the people, the streets, the scenes at the day of East Capital by ZeDuan Zhang, a painter at that time. The painting is about 25 cm in width and 528.7 cm in length, and kept in the Palace Museum in Beijing at the moment.

Based on a sketch about East Capital, in the book the author used West, East, South and North in normal sense, but when he described right or left direction, he was standing in Royal Palace and facing southern direction, which was opposite with the reader's direction. Also East Capital was a huge city, the author definitely could not describe everything and every scene in the city, thus when you read the book, please keep in mind the places or sites described in the book are approximate in the position or in the direction.

Except family name which has already lost its original meaning, every given name in China has its special meaning. As every character has various meanings depending upon occasions and the intention of the developer, it is very difficult to know the exact original meaning or intention for the name, thus we have tried our best to translate the names in the book based on specific circumstance.

It is very interesting to get to know what the biggest capital looked like and what its people were doing at that time, right?

Volume I

———

Outer city of East Capital

The outer city has a perimeter about thirty kilometers, the moat is more than thirty meters wide, the moat is called Protect Dragon River(Hu Lun He), willow trees are planted at the banks of the moat, the walls are white washed with red gates. No pedestrians are allowed to walk along the moat.

At the gate of the outer city, there are three walls including the wall for the outer city, and two half-vat-like walls in front of the gate, one is closer to the wall of the outer city. The closer one is joined to the wall of the outer city, and the other is joined to the closer one, each of the gates for the two half-vat-like walls are located at each side of the gate of the outer city wall. Only South Fragrance Gate(Nan Xun Men), New Zheng Gate (Xin Zheng Men, Xin means new, Zheng is a family name), New Song Men(Xin Song Men) and Qiu's State Gate (Feng Qiu Men, through the gate one could go to the fief of Qiu's family in ancient time) have two walls including the wall of the outer city and only one half-vat-like wall, and the two gates in the walls are kept in a straight line as the emperors need to walk along the way through the gates.

There are three gates at the south side of the outer city: the central gate is called South Fragrance Gate, at southeast side there is Chen Prefecture Gate(Chen Zhou Men which leads to Chen Prefecture), and Cai River is at its side; at southwest side there is Dai Building Gate(Dai Lou Men), and Cai River is at its side too. The official name of Cai River is called BenefitPeople River(Hui Min He), it is called Cai River as it flows from Cai Prefecture.

There are four gates at the east side of the outer city: at the southeast side there is East Water Gate(Dong Shui Men), Bian River flows out of the city through the gate. The gate is located over the river, the gate is wrapped in iron sheet, in night the gate will be lowered down into the river. There is a gate at each side of the river for people's crossing, and there are walls at the both sides of the gate at the east side of the river bank, the walls stretch for more than three hundred meters. From East Water Gate to northern direction, there are New Song Gate(Xin Song Men), New Cao Gate(Xin Cao Men) and Northeast Water Gate(Dong Bei Shui Men) respectively. Fifteen Meters River (Wu Zhang River) flows out Northeast Water Gate from the city.

There are four gates at the west side of the outer city: from south to north there are New Zhen Gate(Xin Zheng Men), West Water Gate(Xi Shui Men), Victories Gate (Wan Sheng Men), Mr. Gu's Gate (Gu Zi Men) and Northwest Water Gate(Xi Bei Shui Men). Bian River flows into the city through West Water Gate, Gold Water River(Jin Shui He) flows into the city through Northwest Water Gate.

There are four gates at the north side of the outer city: from east to west there are Chen's Bridge Gate(Chen Qiao Men), Qiu's State Gate, New Jujube Gate(Xin Suan Zao Men) and Wei Prefecture Gate(Wei Zhou Men). Chen's Bridge Gate is a gate for diplomatic corps of Great Khitan State, Qiu's State Gate is a royal gate for Emperor's procession to pass through when the emperor goes to sacrifice to Earth in north suburb.

The names for the gates are common names used by people, each gate has its own official name, for example West Water Gate is called Benefit Lake(Li Ze Men), New Zheng Gate is called Obeying Heaven Gate(Shun Tian Men), Mr. Gu's Gate is called Golden Glory Gate(Jin Yao Men).

At the top of the wall of the outer city, there are a horse-head-like observation and defense post and an movable defense tower every one hundred and twenty meters, and parapets along the wall. These defense fortifications are maintained daily. When one looks from faraway, the wall and its defense fortifications are high and formidable. Willow and elm trees are planted at both sides of streets within the city, which offer shades to pedestrians. Every two hundred meters along streets there are a warehouse for storing fighting weapons and other necessary tools. There are twenty units with total of ten thousand sappers to maintain and repair the walls, fortifications and streets. There is a commander who is leading the sappers.

Inner City of East Capital

The inner city has a perimeter about 10 kilometers. There are three gates at the south side of the wall of the inner city: the central one is called Rosefinch Gate(Zhu Que Men), the left one is called Preserve Health Gate(Bao Kang Men), and the right one is called New Gate(Xin Men).

There are three gates at the east side of the wall of the inner city: from south to north, at the south bank of Bian River the gate is called Corner Gate(Jiao Zi Men, composed of one water gate and one land gate), at the north bank of Bian River is called Old Song Gate(Jiu Song Men, which is corresponding to New Song Gate of the outer city wall) and Old Cao Gate(Jiu Cao Men, which is corresponding to New Cao Gate of the outer city wall).

There are three gates at the west side of the wall of the inner city: from south to north, they are called Old Zheng Gate(Jiu Zheng Men), Corner Gate at the north bank of Bian River and Pillar Gate (Liang Men), respectively.

There are three gates at the north side of the wall of the inner city: from east to west, they are Old Qiu's State Gate(Jiu Feng Qiu Men, corresponding to Qiu's State Gate of the outer city wall), Revere Dragon Gate (Jin Long Men or Old Jujube Gate (Jiu Suan Zao Men), corresponding to New Jujube Gate) and Golden Water Gate(Jin Shui Men), respectively. Revere Dragon Gate is actually located at the front of a Taoist temple—Revere Dragon Gate(Bao Lu Gong), and the temple is located at the corner of Royal Palace.

Rivers

There are four rivers flowing through East Capital. At the south side it is called Cai River, which flows from Chen and Cai Prefectures into the city through Dai Building Gate at the southwest side of the outer city wall and out of the city through Chen State Gate at the southeast side of the outer city wall. There are eleven bridges along the river within the city: starting from the inside of Chen State Gate, it is called Temple Bridge(Guan Qiao) as it is located at the back of Wu Yue Temple(Wu Yue Qiao, Wu Yue means five highest mountains in China), to north by west direction, it is called Declare Calm Bridge(Xuan Tai Qiao); still to north by west it is called Speedy Horse Bridge (Yun Ji Qiao); still to north by west it is called Horizontal Bridge which is located in the front of the house of Grandma Peng; still to north by west it is called High Bridge; then to west it is called West Bridge of Preserve Health Gate; still to west it is called Dragon Crossing Bridge(Long Jin Qiao), which is just in front of Royal Palace; still to west it is called New Bridge(Xin Qiao); then to south by west it is called Peaceful Bridge(Tai Ping Qiao), which is in front of the mansion of Commander Gao; still to south by west it is called Sell Wheat Bridge(Tiao Mai Qiao); still to south by west it is called First Bridge(Di Yi Zuo Qiao); still to south by west it is called Fit Man Bridge (Yi Nan Qiao), then to the south out of the Dai Building Gate of the outer city it is called Two Kilometers Bridge(Si Li Qiao).

Bian River is at the north of Cai River. Bian River gets its water from the Luo River and Yi River at the outfall of Luo River to Yellow River in West Capital (Luo Yang), flows through East Capital, then flows through Snivel Prefecture City(Si Zhou, the city is buried under a lake at the moment) into Hui River(one of the seven largest rivers in China), grains and other materials from southeast will be transported to East Capital through the river whether for governmental institutions or people.

Three points five kilometers out of East Water Gate to the outside of West Water Gate, there are fourteen bridges along Bian River in East Capital. From east to west, the first bridge is called Rainbow Bridge(Hong Qiao), which is located 3.5 km out of East Water Gate. The bridge is an arch bridge, painted with red pigment, looks like a rainbow. Another two bridges in the river have same structure. Then to west by north it is called Smooth Achievement Warehouse Bridge(Shun Cheng Cang Qiao), then through East Water Gate, still to west by north, there is another bridge inside the outer city, it is called Convenient Bridge(Bian Qiao); still to west by north, it is called Lower Earth Bridge(Xia Tu Qiao); still west by north, it is called Upper Earth Bridge(Shang Tu Qiao); then to west by north through Corner Gate, it is called Assist State Buddhist Temple Bridge(Xiang Guo Si Qiao); still to west by north, it is called Prefecture Bridge(Zhou Qiao) with an official name Milky Way Bridge, which is just at the front of Royal Street of Royal Palace. This bridge and Assist State Buddhist Temple Bridge(Da Xiang Guo Si Qiao) are both low and level, big ships could not pass under the bridges, only small boat with a flat bottom could pass under the bridges. The bridge is supported by bluestone columns, there are balustrades of stone beams and columns at the sides of the bridge. At both banks near the bridge there are stone walls with engraved sea horse, creatures and roaming clouds. There are dense stone columns under the bridge as Royal Carriages will pass through the bridge. At the north bank of the bridge, there is a Royal Street, there are two towering gatehouses at west and east of the street. There are two shallow boats with several long and thick iron spears at the bows at the west of the bridge, there are three iron chains on the bank, in night the boats will be pull out of the water and hung on the surface of the river, in case an upstream ship has a fire, flows down the river, collides with and damage the bridge, threatens the big boats transporting grain and other things and other buildings downstream.

To west by north, it is called Great Rite Bridge(Xun Yi Qiao); still west by north, it is called Vitalize State Buddhist Temple Bridge(Xing Guo Si Qiao), and is also called Cavalry Headquarter Bridge(Ma Bing Ya Men Qiao); still west by north, it is called Prime Minister Mansion Bridge(Tai Shi Fu Qiao), it is located in front of the mansion of Prime Minister Cai; still west by north, it is called Gold Beam Bridge(Jin Liang Qiao); still west by north, it is called Pontoon Bridge(Fu Qiao), in past the bridge was constructed with ships, at the moment it is constructed with stone and wood; still west by north, it is called Convenient Bridge at West Water Gate (Xi Shui Men Bian Qiao); still west by north, outside of West Water Gate, it is called Horizontal Bridge(Heng Qiao).

Fifteen Meters River flows through the northeastern part of the capital. The river flows from Ji and Yun Prefectures, grains and other things from East Capital Province (Jing Dong Lu) are transported into the capital by the river, the river flows into the capital at the north side of New Cao Gate. There are five bridges across the river; from west to east, the first one is called Little Horizontal Bridge(Xiao Heng Qiao); still to east by south, it is called Full Preparation Bridge (Guang Bei Qiao); still to east by south, it is Cai Market Bridge(Cai Shi Qiao); still to east by south, it is called Dim Light Bridge(Qin Hui Qiao); still to east by south, it is called Dye House Bridge(Ran Yuan Qiao).

Gold Water River (Jin Shui He) flows through the northwestern part of the capital, the river gets its water from Jin and Suo Rivers located at the southwest direction of the capital through diversion canal and wooden flume, flows over Bian River and into the capital at Northwest Water Gate, then into the royal garden of the Palace through high walls. There are three bridges along the river, from west to east, they are called White Tiger Bridge(Bai Hu Qiao), Horizontal Bridge(Heng Qiao) and Five Kings Bridge(Wu Wang Qiao). Gold Water River flows out of the capital at Old Cao Gate.

There is a branch of Gold Water River flowing around Royal Palace from west to south by west direction, then the branch flows out of the royal palace and into the moat around the palace. The segment of Gold Water River from the royal palace moat to Old Cao Gate is called Little River(Xia He Zi), there is a bridge over Little River, it is called Cao Gate Little River Bridge(Cao Men Xia He Zi Qiao) and also called Nembutsu Bridge(Nian Fo Qiao). All the palanquin bearers, retinues etc. of Royal Palace stayed at barracks outside of Old Cao Gate, in early morning they will go to the palace through the bridge to work. When they pass through the bridge, there is always blind person praying to Buddha and begging alms.

Royal Palace

The main gate of Royal Palace is called Declare Kindness Building(Xuan De Lou). There are five gates in the building, the gates are all painted red and adorned with golden nails. The walls around the building are made of bricks and stones, and dragons, phoenixes and roaming clouds are engraved onto the walls. There are carved ridges, painted beams and rafters, layered eaves with glazed tiles everywhere. The buildings are very high. There are two buildings at the side of Declare Kindness Building which look like a carpenter's square, the two buildings are also adorned with red balustrades. There is one pavilion each at the foot of the two buildings, and red wood barricade in front of each pavilion to prevent and control passing through of people and horses.

One comes to Grand Celebration Hall(Da Qin Dian) through the main gate further north. There is one each side hall at the east and west side of Grand Celebration Hall, the side hall looks like bell tower in a temple, an office of Grand Astrology Administration is in the side hall, the staffs on duty will observe, check and maintain hourglass. They will report time every fifteen minutes and every hour to the officials on duty in the palace. Important ceremonies and grand assembly in January first will be held in the hall, so does the emperor for his own fasting. There is a gate at each left and right side of the hall. They are called Left Grand Celebration Gate and Right Grand Celebration Gate(Zuo You Da Qing Men).

There are three gates at the south side of the palace wall, which are used for the ministers to go to offices. At the left side of Declare Kindness Building is called Left Gate, the right side Right Gate. You will come to Comprehend Hall through Left Gate, the hall is also called for Administration Hall(Ming Tang, many activities such as morning session,celebration, awarding ceremony, and worship ceremony are held in the hall instead of Grand Celebration Hall). When you go through Right Gate, you go to west and will come across buildings called Heaven Papers(Tian Zhang, for storing papers, books and articles for emperors), Treasured Articles(Bao Wen, for storing papers, books and articles for emperors) etc. There are about three hundred meters from the palace wall to North Corridor(Bei Lang); you go to east, at the north side of the street, you will come to Ministry of Defense(Shu Mi Yuan); General Office for issuing Imperial Edict and getting reports from other officials to Emperor(Zhong Shu Sheng); Prime Minister's Office(Du Tang), he will work in the office after the morning session with Emperor; Ministry of Evaluation and Approval(Men Xia Sheng, an office responsible for checking the appropriateness of various decrees and reports); then you come to the side gate of the corridor at the side of Grand Celebration Hall.

You will come to the second side gate three hundred meters further north through the side gate of the corridor at the side of Grand Celebration Hall, every morning when prime minister and ministers come to morning session, they have to dismount at this gate; other officials who come to morning session have to dismount at the first side gate of the corridor at the side of Grand Celebration Hall and walk to the second side gate. All officials walk to Ideal Moral Hall(Wen De Dian). When you come through the second side gate, at the east corridor it is the east side gate of Grand Celebration Hall; at the west corridor there are inner offices for General Office and Ministry of Evaluation and Approval(Zhong Shu Men Xia Hou Sheng), then National History Institute(Xiu Guo Shi Yuan), then South Side Corner Gate(Nan Xiang Xiao Jiao Men), which is just across Ideal Moral Hall, in which Emperor holds morning session. There is one street behind Ideal Moral Hall and Grand Celebration Hall from west to east. At the east end of the street there is a gate called East Magnificent Gate(Dong Hua Men), at the west end West Magnificent Gate(Xi Hu Men). Inside East and West Magnificent Gates there is another pair of symmetric gates located at the sides of the halls called Left and Right Solemn Praise Gates(Zuo You Jia Su Men), respectively, further inside Left and Right Solemn Praise Gates, there is another pair of symmetric gates called Left and Right Silver Tower Gates(Zuo You Yin Tai Men), respectively.

The palace of crown prince is located inside East Magnificent Gate, from the palace you enter Solemn Praise Gate, the back gate of Grand Celebration Hall and at East and West Side Gates of Ideal Moral Hall are at the south side of the street; Declare Bless Gate(Xuan You Men) is at the north side of the street. When you go through Declare Bless Gate, you will come to a west corridor in south to north direction. There is a palace called Gaze Sunshine Hall(Nin Hui Dian) facing eastern direction. There is a gate called Assemble Pass Gate(Hui Tong Men), through the gate you will go into the working area of Emperor. In the east corridor across Gaze Sunshine Hall, there are six departments for food, medicine, liquor, clothes, house, and palanquin and carriages to provide service for the inner palaces(Dian Zhong Shen Liu Shang Ju) and royal kitchen(Yu Chu). There are two security lines within Gaze Sunshine Hall on high alert to guard inner palaces to check people going in and coming out of the inner palaces. The eunuchs trusted by emperors and could walk around the inner palaces are guarding inner security line and stay in the palace. Other people such as royal doctors and eunuch officials on duty are waiting outside Gaze Sunshine Hall. Heralds(Kuai Xing), retinues (Qin Cong Guan), bearers of palanquin(Nian Guan), cleaners (Huang Yuan Zi), internal guards (Nei Zhu Si Bing Shi), ceremony masters(Zhi Hou) etc. who are waiting in the place on call. All things purchased by Inner Palaces and tributes from other places are sent into Inner Palaces through the place, thus a lot of people are working in the place. Inner Palaces purchase a lot of unique things and foods which are rarely seen in ordinary market. When Emperor has his breakfast, lunch and super, guards are standing from inner palaces to Gaze Sunshine Hall to prevent unrelated people passing around. A person in charge of Emperor's food called 'Bo Shi Jia' will issue order, then men with violet clothes and head scarf called 'Yuan Zi Jia' will go forward with a food box in right hand and a red embroidered silk handkerchief in his left hand through the place. Each box is covered with a yellow cover embroidered with dragon, there are a dozen of such kind of boxes each time. Then the boxes are followed by more than twenty golden melon shaped boxes to supplement food on temporary order, the boxes are called 'Fan Suo'.

You will come to Polaris Hall when you go to west direction out of Declare Bless Gate at the north side, at January First, Emperor will accept congratulations from his ministers in the hall; at the south side, you will come to Ideal Moral Hall, Emperor holds morning session in the hall; at the west side of Polaris Hall(Zi Chen Dian), you will come to Easy Administration Hall (Chui Gong Dian), Emperor holds his informal discussion with his senior ministers in the hall; at the west side of Easy Administration Hall, you will come to Royal Rite Hall(Huang Yi Dian), which is a place for funeral; at the west side of Royal Rite Hall, you will come to Gather Outstanding People Hall(Ji Ying Dian), Emperor holds royal banquet and examines the scholars who have already passed imperial examination by himself in the hall; at the back of Royal Rite Hall, you will come to Commander Test Hall (Chong Zheng Dian), Emperor holds face interview with generals and senior commander in the hall; at the back of Gather Outstanding People Hall, you will come to Preserve Hall(Bao He Dian), the hall is with a splendid garden of various trees and pond with artificial hills of unique stones from other places of the country, Emperor will host banquets for his senior ministers, royal highness and his queen and concubines in the hall; at the back of the inner palaces, there is a study room for Emperor called Careful Thinking Hall (Rui Si Dian), Emperor studies and takes his food in the hall; the back gate of Royal Palace is called Guard Dragon Gate(Gong Chen Men).

There is a prosperous market out of East Magnificent Gate as many things for inner palaces are purchased from the market. Many things are sold in the market including foods, drinks, fresh seasonable fruits and flowers, fish, shrimp, crab, turtle, quail and rabbit, other cured meats from wild animals, gold and jade jewelry, antiques, and clothes etc. All are the most treasured and valuable things from all over the country. The vegetables and meats are in dozens of kinds. If someone needs more than a dozen dishes, the materials could be bought in the market at any time. When new seasonable vegetables and fruits, eggplants and squash etc. are brought into market, a pair of eggplant and squash could worth more than 3000 to 5000 bronze coins(one thousand coins could buy sixty kilos rice at that time), and concubines of Emperor will rush to purchase at higher price.

Inner Service Departments Of Royal Palace

Inner Service Departments are located within Royal Palace. The departments include: Secretariat(Xue Shi Yuan); Royal Guard(Huang Cheng Si); Ritual Office(Si Fang Guan); Reception Office(Ke Shen);Security Check Offices(Dong Xi Shang Ge Men) at east and west sides of the south corridor of Polaris Hall to check people going into Inner Palace; Materials Check Office(Tong Jin Si) for checking reports and papers to Emperor from Ministries and Officials and sending the reports and papers back after the comments or approvals of Emperor; Armories(Wu Ku) for Bow and Arrow, Sword, Spear and Armour; Liquor and Tea Office(Han Lin Si); Internal Imperial Edict Service(Nei Si Shen) for passing imperial edict by eunuchs; Royal Treasury(Nei Cang Ku); Imperial Articles Depot(Feng Chen Ku) for storing silk, gold, silver and other valuables; Great Luck Hall Depot(Jing Fu Dian Ku) for storing silk, gold, silver and other tributes of other countries; Prolong Luck Hall(Yan Fu Gong), which is an independent special depot outside of Royal Palace for storing silk, gold, silver and silk for rewarding military exploit; Concubines Office for administrations of various houses occupied by Emperor's concubines; Spice and Perfume Depot; Manufacturing and Repairing Shop in charge of manufacturing and repairing various things needed in Royal Palace such as for dying, knitting, preparing paint, sewing waist bands etc.; Writing Paper and Brushing Office for supplying books, writing papers, writing brushes, ink, inkstand, chess and musical instrument; Medical Office for taking care of patients in Royal Palace and taking care of other ministers by imperial order and administering medical service of whole country; Heaven Papers(Tian Zhang) and Treasured Articles(Bao Wen) are used as two places for storing papers, books and articles of emperors; Administration Hall Office(Ming Tang Ban Su Bu Zheng Fu) in charge of announcing calendar for next year and imperial laws and regulations.

Outer Service Departments of Royal Palace

Outer Service Departments of Royal Palace include: Right and Left Guard of Honor Departments (Zou and You Jin Wu Jie Zhang Si) in charge of clearing way, setting up guard of honor and maintaining the order of the occasion when Emperor goes out to have tour of inspection and other activities; Official Distillery Shop(Fa Jiu Ku) in charge of making liquors for Emperor, sacrifice and bestowing; Internal Distillery Shop(Nei Jiu Ku) in charge of making liquors for territorial states; Cattle and Sheep Department(Niu Yang Si) in charge of providing beef and mutton and other meats; Milk and Cheese House(Ru Lao Yuan) in charge of providing milk and cheese; Imperial Carriage Department (Yi Luan Si) in charge of palanquin for sending Emperor to morning session, banquet, worship and sacrifice ceremonies, inspection tour etc.; Carriage Department(Che Luo Yuan) in charge of providing carriages according to occasion; Tribute Depot(Gong Feng Ku) in charge of storing tributes from the annual tribute of all the provinces; Disposal Office(Za Mai Wu) in charge of disposing of excess materials; East and West Manufacturing Shops(Dong Xi Zuo Fang) in charge of manufacturing weapons; All Weaponry Manufacturing Shop(Wan Quan Zuo Fang) in charge of manufacturing weapons for Royal Palace; Maintenance Department(Xiu Nei Si) in charge of maintenance of Royal Palace and other sacrifice places such Imperial Ancestors Temple; Upper and Lower Civil Manufacturing Shops(Wen Si Yuan Shang Xia Jie), Upper Shop is in charge of manufacturing valuables of gold, silver, jade and pearl etc. and Lower Shop in charge of manufacturing daily articles of damask silk, brocade, lacquer, wooden, bronze, iron, official seals and certificates for monk and nun etc.; Brocade And Damask Silk House (Ling Jin Yuan) in charge of manufacturing damask silk, brocade, silk gauze, crepe, yarn, thin and tough silk for Emperor's clothes; Embroidering House (Wen Xiu Yuan) in charge of embroidering

Emperor's clothes and other materials such as cover of carriage and banners etc.; Weaponry Administration Department(Jun Qi Suo) in charge of weapon manufacturing; Upper and Lower Bamboo and Wood Tax Department(Shang and Xia Zhu Mu Wu) in charge of collecting tax on bamboo and wood; Mat Tax Department (Bo Chang) in charge of collecting tax on reed and bamboo mat; Carriage Supporting Department (Che Ying) in charge of raising donkey and cattle for pulling carriages; Long Distance Supporting Department(Zhi Yuan Wu) in charge of raising donkey and mules for pulling carriages; Mule Department (Luo Wo); Camel House (Tuo Fang) in charge of raising camel; Elephant House (Xiang Yuan) in charge of raising and training elephants for grand sacrifice ceremony in south suburb; Raw Materials Depot of Weaponry(Zuo Fang Wu Liao Ku) in charge of supplying raw materials such iron, wood, lead, tin, leather, wax and feather etc.; East and West Kiln Service Departments(Dong Xi Yao Wu) in charge of making bricks, tiles and other materials; Inner Food Supply House (Nei Wu Ku) in charge of rice, wheat flour, sugar, honey, date, bean,oil etc. for Royal Palace and Outer Food Supply House (Wai Wu Ku) in charge of oil, salt, rice and flour etc. for other governmental institutions out of Royal Palace; Oil and Vinegar Depot (You Cu Ku) in charge of sesame oil, rapeseed oil, perilla oil and vinegar; Capital Defense Weaponry Administration (Jing Cheng Shou Ju Suo) in charge of storing weapons on the top of city walls to defend the capital; Saddle, Rein and Bridle Depot (An Pei Ku) in charge of using royal horse, saddle, rein and bridle; Left and Right Steed Houses (Zuo You Qi Ji Yuan) in charge of raising horses; 10 Markets of Coal Monopoly Bureaus at South and North Bank of Bian River(He Nan He Bei Shi Tan Chang) in charge of selling coals; Four Pharmacies of Prepared Medicine Monopoly Bureau(Si Shu Yao Ju) in charge of selling prepared medicine for ordinary people at four places in East, South, West and North of the capital; Internal and External Firewood Depot(Nei Wai Chai Tan Ku) in charge of supplying firewood to Royal Palace and other places, respectively; Military Officer Recommendation Department(Jun Tou Yin Jian Si) in charge of recommending military leaders to have face interview and martial arts demonstration for Emperor, and so do other military army commanders when they return from battlefield; House Leasing Department(Jia ZI Ying) in charge of leasing, rent collecting, maintaining and developing all public houses; Tea Monopoly Bureau(Que Huo Wu Du Cha Chang) in charge of issuing licenses for transporting and selling of tea; Imperial Clan Affairs Bureau (Da Zong Zheng Shi) in charge of affairs related to imperial clan whether civil or criminal affairs; Left Treasury (Zuo Zang) in charge of booking tax and paying salary to officials and soldiers; Grand Bank(Da Guan) in charge of storing coins, silver, gold and jewelry; Prime Warehouse (Yuan Feng) in charge of storing coins, jade, etc.; Assessment and Disposal Bureau (Bian Gu Ju) in charge of assessing and appraising of perfumes and spices and other confiscated materials to be sold by Disposal Office; Sale House (Da Tao Suo) in charge of disposing of spice and perfumes and other materials unused in Royal Palace.

For rice and wheat granaries: near Rainbow Bridge at the east side of the capital, there are Primary Granary(Yuan Feng Cang, it was reported more than twenty four thousand tons grains were stored in the granary); Great Harvest Granary (Shun Cheng Cang); within East Water Gate, there are Vast Aid Granary (Guang Ji Cang), Inner River and Outer River Intermediary Granaries (Businessmen would get money, tea, salt, spice from the granaries for grains, fodders or money they have deposited along the border areas or the capital), Wealthy Nation Granary (Fu Guo Cang), Great Surplus Granary (Guang Ying Cang), Plenty Surplus Granary (Wan Ying Cang), Forever Harvest Granary(Yong Feng Cang), Distant Aid Granary (Ji Yuan Cang) etc.; within Chen Prefecture Gate, Wheat Granary(Mai Cang Ji); in north of the capital, Yi Mount Granary (Yi Shan Cang), Fifteen Meters River Granaries including Grand Storage Granary(Guang Chu Cang) and Grand Accumulation Granary (Guang Ji Cang) etc. There are total about fifty granaries in the capital. Grains are transported and taken out the granaries by soldiers under Loading and Unloading Department(Zhi Na Xia Xie Si) of the army; the grains would be carried by special handlers after the soldiers take the grains out of the granary by carrying two bags. In the day when grains are sent out, the place is bustling like a marketplace.

Not faraway from the capital, there are more than twenty places for storing animal fodder(Cao Liao Chang). When winter comes, the ox carts from other places to send fodders and grains will fill the streets around the place, the animal fodder are piled like mountain. When army get their grains and animal fodders, they have to take the grains and animal fodder by themselves and are not allowed to hire other people to help, which is a regulation promulgated by First Emperor (Tai Zu) and Second Emperor (Tai Zong) of the dynasty.

Volume Two

Royal Streets

The royal street in front of Declare Kindness Building goes to south direction with a width of more than three hundred meters. At the sides of royal street, there are royal corridors, before businessmen were allowed to do business within the corridors, since 1111 AD, no more business is allowed in the corridors. The black wood barricades are set up in front of the corridors, two lines of red wood barricades are set up in the royal street. No pedestrians and carriages are allowed to pass through the royal street. Pedestrians could only walk under the corridor outside of the black wood barricades. Inside the black wood barricades there is a royal ditch layered by bricks and stones at each side of the royal street, lotus are planted since 1119 AD. Along the banks of the royal ditch peach, plum, pear, apricot and other fruit trees and other flowers are planted. In spring and summer various flowers are booming alternately, when one looks from faraway, it just looks like a painted beautiful picture.

Official Residences of Various Ministries in Front of Declare Kindness Building

In front of Declare Kindness Building across Left Side Gate of the building, there is left corridor extending from north to south, at the outside of the corridor there are Administration Hall Office in charge of announcing calendar for next year and imperial laws and regulations and National Library in charge of books, history, archives, calendar etc.; across Right Side Gate, there is right corridor extending from north to south, at the outside of the corridor in east side there are eight official residences for Ministry of Defense(Shu Mi Yuan) and General Office for issuing Imperial Edict and getting reports from other officials to Emperor(Zhong Shu Sheng); in west side there is State Council (Shang Shu Sheng) in charge of ministries. Along Royal Street (the wide street of more than 300 meters in front of Declare Kindness Building) further south, there are East and West Imperial Ancestors Temples at the sides of the street for hanging and worshiping portraits of all dead emperors and empresses; further south, there is Grand Prosperity House at the east side of the street in charge of ceremonial music; further south, near Prefecture Bridge, there is Great Norms House at the east side of the street in charge of rituals for sacrifice to God of Land and God of Grain, various temples etc.

Left Coin Depot (Zuo Cang Ku) is located at the corner in the street of Prefecture Bridge, the depot is facing south direction. At the east side of the depot, there is Prime Minister Zheng's mansion, fish shop and meat shop. From the south gate of East Imperial Ancestors Palace to east, at the south side there are Tang's gold and silver and jewelry shop, Wen Zhou lacquerware and grocery shop, Assist State Buddhist Temple, Thirteen Room Warehouse and Lodging Hotel near Old Song Gate. Across West Imperial Ancestors Temple in diagonally opposite direction, there is a street called Return Kindness Temple Street, there are General Post Office(Du Jin Zou Yuan) in charge of receiving and sending official documents all over the country, a pharmacy, fruit shops and cake shops till to Great Rite Bridge Street. At the north of Prefecture Bridge West Street(Zhou Qiao Xi Da Jie), there is Capital Guest House(Du Ting Yi) for accepting envoys of Great Khitan State, across Guest House it is Liang's jewelry shop and various shops for papers, fruits and flowers. At the west side of Great Rite Bridge Street, it is Municipal Government of Capital(Kai Feng Fu).

Further south along Royal Street after crossing Prefecture Bridges, there are residential buildings at the sides of the street. At the east side are Che's Coal, Zhang's Liquor, Wang's plum flower like steamed stuffed bun, Grandma Cao's meat pie, Fourth Li's tea house, till Rosefinch Gate. At the west side it is called Liquor House Street. Meet Immortal Headquarter Restaurant(Yu Xian Zheng Dian, one of the famous restaurants in the capital) is located at the south side of the street. There is a marquee in front of the restaurant, there are pavilions and stages at the back of the restaurant, it is called On Stage (Tai Shang) by people of the capital. It is one of the best restaurants in the capital, four liters liquor in silver bottle costs 72 bronze coins, four liters lamb liquor(Yang Gao Jiu, the liquor is fermented with cooked mutton meat, fat and soup and rice, one of the expensive liquors at that time) costs 81 bronze coins. At the north side of the street, there are a branch store of Xue's Tea House, a restaurant for serving rice with cooked mutton, a shop for cooked mutton. Further west, there are brothels, it is called Brothel Street (Yuan Jie) by people. At the west side of the royal corridor, there are Lu's Steamed Stuffed Bun, tea houses, restaurants for porridge, tea houses, liquor shops, spice and perfume shops and residential buildings.

Streets and Alleys Out of Rosefinch Gate

When you comes out of Rosefinch Gate, there are residential buildings at east side of Royal Street. It is called Wheat Straw Street to east direction, there is Number One Scholar Hotel (Zhuang Yuan Lou, providing lodging for students from other places to take part in imperial examination in the capital, the number one person of the examination will be given a title of Number One Scholar by Emperor and appointed to a high position), all remaining buildings are brothels till to Preserve Health Street(Bao Kang Men Jie). At the west side of Royal Street out of Rosefinch Gate to west you will come to Entertainment Street(Xin Men Wa Zi, for theaters, brothels, gambling houses), to south it is called Pig Butchering Alley, a lot of brothels are located in the alley. Further south, there are two Music Rehearsal Halls(Jiao Fang, in charge of all musics except for rituals), remaining are residential buildings or tea houses. The business in the area are prosperous, particularly in night.

When you come out of Dragon Crossing Bridge and goes to south direction along the royal street, you will see Red Wooden Barricades in the street again, like in front of Royal Palace. At the east side you will see Inspector General Liu's Mansion(Liu Lian Fang Zhai); further south you will see Ministry of Education and its affiliated university(Guo Zi Jian, in accepting children of officials at or above seventh grade in rank and administering educational affairs of the country); further south you will see National University (Tai Xue, in accepting children of officials at or below Eighth Grade in rank and excellent children of ordinary people); further south, you will cross another street, the south gate of National University is located at the street. At the south side of the street, you will see South Branch Office of Prepared Medicine Monopoly Bureau (Shu Yao Hui Min Nan Ju). From the south branch office, all are residential buildings for about

2.5 km and you will come to another street running from west to east direction. The street is the street of the back gate of Wu Yue Temple(Wu Yue Guan). From the back gate, you go about 250 meters, you will come to Street Watch Pavilion(Kan Jie Ting), when Emperor come to the place, he will stand at the top of the pavilion to watch pedestrians and carriages walking in streets. You go further east along the street, you will come to warehouse of National Examination Center(Gong Yuan Shi Wu Ku), Evaluation Center of Ministry of Personnel (Li Bu Gong Yuan in charge of evaluating and maintaining of personal files and examination papers regarding candidates who have already passed imperial examinations at county, province and national levels), Carriage Department(Che Wu Ying, in charge of providing ox, donkeys and carriages for various governmental departments), Animal Fodder Warehouse(Cao Liao Chang). At the south of the street, you will see Preserve Genuineness Taoist Temple(Bao Zhen Gong), which extends to Speedy Horse Bridge of Bian River. From Royal Street to the inside street (Li Jie) of South Fragrance Gate, the most grand building is Wu Yue Temple. From the west gate of Wu Yue Temple to east, you will come to Temple Bridge, Declare Calm Bridge, there is a shady street which extends for about 2.5 km. Within the area, there are a Temple for Praying to Ten Gods of Heaven(Zhong Tai Yi Gong, when one prays to the gods, there will be no wars, no pestilence in the land) and Blessing God Temple(You Shen Guan), at the south side of the street there are Meet Soul Temple(Ming Li Dian), Dedicate Soul Garden(Feng Ling Yuan, one of the parks in the capital), Nine Cauldrons Palace (Jiu Cheng Gong, there are nine cauldrons with water and earth picked from nine prefectures in the palace to symbolize the sovereignty over the places). No faraway at east side you will come Greet Luck Lake, weeping willows are planted around the banks, different lotus flowers, wild rices and cattails are planted in the lake, mallards and wild goose and other water fowls are floating and playing onto the lake, there are bridges, pavilions, stages, high towers around the lake. Ordinary people could only visit the park in Tomb Sweeping Day(Qin Ming Jie).

When you come out of Dragon Crossing Bridge and goes to south direction along the royal street, at the west side of Royal Street, you will come across Privy Councillor Deng's Mansion. Further south, within the alley of Military School(Wu Xue), you will come to famous opera singer Zhang's house and Great Grandfather's Temple(Wu Cheng Wang Miao, for worshiping famous strategist TaiGong Jiang of Zhou Dynasty 1128-1016 BC and other famous generals in history), further south you will come to Zhang's Deep-fried Dough Cake, then Empress Ming Jie's Former House before she became Empress. To west you will come to a wide street called Big Alley Entrance(Da Xiang Kou), further west, you will come to Cool Breeze Restaurant, many residents of the capital will cool down in the area during summer night. Further west you will come to Old Crow Alley Entrance, there is an arms depot, which extends to First Bridge. From the entrance to south, you will come to Prolong Genuineness Taoist Temple(Yan Zhen Guan) to receive Taoist disciples coming to the capital from all over the country. From the south of the temple, you to go west, you will come to Buddhist Academy(San Xue Yuan). Further west, you will come to a small alley near Fit Man Bridge.

You go to south further along Royal Street, you will come to South Fragrance Gate. Funeral procession is not allowed to pass through the gate whether for an official family or an ordinary family. It is said as the gate directly leads to Royal Palace. Only pigs from other places to Capital have to pass through the gates. Every night tens thousands pigs are driven into the city by dozens of people, no pigs would run in disorderly fashion.

From Prefecture Bridge to Dragon Crossing Bridge, along Royal Street, some people sell rice porridge, meat roasted in fresh cinders and jerky at side of the street. In front of Jade Building(Yu Lou) people sell badger meat, fox meat and air-dried chickens. Mei's and Lu's shops sell cooked goose, duck, chicken and rabbit meat, intestine, lung, eel, steamed stuffed bun, chicken skin, kidney, entrails. Every kind of meat costs less than fifteen coins per portion. Cao's deserts are also sold in the place.

When you come to Rosefinch Gate, people sell fried sheep intestine filled with blood on the spot, cured or fermented fish, fermented soybean with ginger, cooked thin slices of meat, cooked sliced pig and sheep innards, cooked sheep blood mixed with wheat flour, sliced cooked sheep head meat, spicy pig and sheep feet and spicy radish with ginger. In summer people sell chicken skin with sesame-starch mixture looking like bean curd, jellied sesame-starch mixture looking like jellied bean curd, fried vegetables, ice-cold sugared meat ball, sugared Chinese honey locust seed, sugar preserved papaya, medical papaya, gorgon fruit, cold sugared green pea licorice water, lychee paste, preserved turnip, pickled vegetable, apricot, sugared plum with chopped ginger and basil, lettuce, bamboo shoot, mustard spicy cucumber, fried stuffed round flour cake, deserts, assorted sugar preserved lychee, cranberry, basil paste, preserved plum, orange, all are packed in plum-color box. In winter, people sell shredded rabbit meat with noodle, roasted pork with skin on the spot, mallard meat, cooked cold carp seasoned with vinegar and chopped green onions and garlic, fried stuffed flapjack, pig entrails. People sell various foods along the street till to Dragon Crossing Bridge. All these foods are called 'Miscellaneous Chewy', and are sold till late at night.

Streets and Alleys Near East Turret

When you go to east from Declare Kindness Building, you will come to East Turret at the southeast corner of Royal Palace. You go through a crossroad, go to south, you come to Ginger Shop, and High Head

Street (Gao Tou Jie); you go to north, you come to yarn shop and to street out of East Magnificent Gate, further north, you come to Morning Glow Gate(Chen Hui Men), there are so many shops along the way till Old Jujube Gate, it is one of the busiest areas in the capital. The streets are expanded between 1119-1125 AD.

When go to east from the crossroad, you will come to Fan's Restaurant Street. At the south side of the street, you come to an eagle and gyrfalcon shop, the shop only provides lodging for the eagle and gyrfalcon peddlers. Other shops sell pearls, cloth, spice and perfume. Further to south, you will come Ordination Alley(Jie Shen Xiang), the alley is a market for gold, silver and silk. The buildings are magnificent and tall, shop fronts are elegant and resplendent, the buildings are next to each other. Business might involve ten million coins for one transaction, when you witness the scene, you will get pretty shocked.

You go to east from Ordination Alley, you come to Pan's Restaurant at the north side of the alley. Near the restaurant from 5 o'clock in morning, people begin to sell clothes, paintings, rare articles, rhinoceros horn and jade. At daybreak, people begin to sell sheep's head, animal intestine and lung, kidney, testes, breast, bovine stomach and lung, quail, rabbit, turtledove, pigeon, other wild fowls, crab, clam and other seafood. After the market is over, people begin to sell materials for handicraft men. After lunch, various foods such as cheese, cake with jujube, steamed red bean bun, sugar preserved fruit, carved sugar preserved fruit etc. In evening people begin to sell counterfeit head-dress(Tou Mian), head comb(Guan Shu)(A decoration article used for hairs), laced long collars for women's clothes(Ling Mo), rare articles and daily necessities. Further east, you come to Xu's Vegetable Porridge Shop (Besides vegetable porridge, it will also sell fried bean curd, fish, eggplant etc.).

You go to east from Ordinary Alley, you come to Sang's Comprehensive Recreation Center(Sang Jia Wa Zi), near north side of Sang's Center is Middle Center(Zong Wa Zi), to south side of Sangs Center is Inner Center(Li Wa Zi). There are more than fifty stages and other shops in the centers. Lotus House and Peony House in Middle Center and Yaksha House and Elephant House in Inner Center are the biggest ones, each could hold about one thousand audience, since famous comic artists AppearFirst Ding(XianXian Ding), OneMass Wangt(TuanZi Wang) and SeventhSage Zhang(QiSheng Zhang) played in the centers, many players come to the centers to play. In the centers some people sell used clothes, drugs, do fortune telling, do wrestling, sell foods and drinks, do haircut, do paper flower cutting, do singing etc. You can play all day long in the centers, without your awareness, it is dark.

Streets and Alleys East of Pan's Restaurant

You go east from Pan's Restaurant till a crossroad, the area is called Bamboo Pole Market(Zhu Gan Shi or Tu Shi Zi, bustling market for selling bamboo pole).

From Bamboo Pole Market further east till a crossroad, the area is called Corner Tea Shop Area(Cong Guo Jiao Cha Fang). People begin to do business starting from 3 o'clock in morning with lamp. People sell clothes, paintings, garlands, laced long collars for women's clothes. The business ends at daybreak, thus it is called 'ghost market'.

You go further east from 'ghost market', at the north side of the street, you come to HundredThousands Zhao's house. At the south side of the street, you come to Central Mountain (Zhong Shan)Headquarter Restaurant which is one of the seventy two famous restaurants in the capital; then you come to East and West Elm Forest Alleys. At the north side of the street, you come to Empress Zheng's former house. At the corner of the east end of the street to north wall, you come to Temple of General Shan and his tomb(One of the famous generals at the end of Sui Dynasty 581-618 AD). There is a jujube tree in the graveyard. It is said the tree coming from his jujube wood spear, thus the alley is called 'Jujube Grave Alley'(Zao Zhong Zi Xiang).

From General Shan's Tomb further east, you come to Old Cao Gate. At the north side of the street, you come to Hill Tea House(Shan Zi Cha Fang). There are Immortal Caves and Bridges in the house. Many women of noblemen and officials go to the house to have tea in night for fun. Further east you come to Lettuce Li's Children Pharmacy(Li Sheng Cai Xiao Er Yao Pu) and Area Commander Qiu's Pharmacy (Maybe the ancestor of the owner was once an area commander).

When you come out of Old Cao Gate, you come to Zhu's Bridge Recreational Center(Zhu Jia Qiao Wa Zi). You come down the bridge, you come to South and North Byways(Nan Bei Xie Jie), there are a Mount Tai Temple and brothels in the streets. There are a lot of people doing business around the bridge, the business is not a bit less than the area around Prefecture Bridge. Further east, you come to Ox Walk Street (Niu Xing Jie), famous Liu's Pharmacy(Xia Ma Liu Jia Yao Pu) is located in the street, so does Ox Watch Restaurant. There are also brothels in the area till to New City.

If you go south from Bamboo Pole Market, you come to Israel Restaurant(Tie Xue Lou Jiu Dian, one of the 72 famous restaurants in the capital). Further south, you come to Emperor's Residence(before he became an emperor, Huang Jian Yuan) Street. Zhen's Fried Pancake Shop is located in the street, there are more than twenty pots and stoves making the pancake at the same time. Further south, you come to Imperial Ancestors Temple(Tai Miao) street, Bright Sunshine Headquarter Restaurant (Gao Yang Zheng Dian, one of the seventy two famous restaurants in the capital) is located in the street, the night market is very famous one in the capital.

If you go north from Bamboo Pole Market, you come to Horse Walk Avenue(Ma Xing Jie), there are a lot of people walking and doing business along the avenue. You will come to a crossroad, the area is called Wren Market (Liao Er Shi). From the crossroad, you go to east, you come to East Prostitute Alley, you go to west, you come to West Prostitute Alley, brothels are located in the alleys; you go to north, you come to Yang's Restaurant Street(Yang Lou Jie) , at the east side of the street, you come to Zhuang's Restaurant (It is Make Harmony Restaurant(He Yue Lou) at the moment, one of the seventy two famous restaurants in the capital) , there is a horse market near the restaurant. The nearest restaurant at the north of Zhuang's Restaurant, it is called Ren's Restaurant(It is called Happy Melody Restaurant(Xin Yue Lou) at the moment, one of the seventy two famous restaurants in the capital). Across street it is Ma's Griddle Porridge Shop.

Restaurants

Nearly every restaurant in the capital has a marquee in front of the restaurant, except Ren's Restaurant. When you enter the gate of the restaurant, you will enter a long corridor about one hundred fifty meters, the corridor is connected by courtyards at south and north ends, there are many private rooms along the sides of the corridor. In night, the rooms both at upstairs and downstairs are brightly lit with lanterns and candles, everything looks splendid under the lights. Several hundred prostitutes with heavy makeup would stand along the corridor to wait for customers to pick them up. When you look from faraway, they all look like fairies.

You go north further from Ren's Restaurant, cross Horse Walk Street, you will come to two alleys, they are called Large and Small Handicraft Shops Alleys(Da Xiao Huo Hang), handicraft men live in these alleys. Small Handicraft Shop Alley is connected to brothels of Prostitute Alleys, and Large Handicraft Shop Alley is connected to Stationery Shops.

Alum Building(Pan's Restaurant) which is called Harvest Happiness Building was rebuilt in the period between 1119-1125 AD. The restaurant has five buildings, each building is three-storey high, the five buildings stand independently and are connected by suspension bridge with balustrades, each room has a bead curtain with embroidered room label over the door, under light the curtain is shining colorfully. When the restaurant just opened, in first two days it would give a gold banner to each customer. In Lantern Festival, the restaurant will put lotus-shaped lanterns on each column of titles on the roof. Later West Building of the restaurant does not allow people to go out to overlook at the third floor as people could look down into Royal Palace.

Whether it is cold or hot day, whether it is rainy or windy day, restaurants of the capital open early and close late every day with bustling business.

Out of Old Song Gate at east side of the capital, there are Love Harmony Restaurant(Ren He Dian) and Jiang's Restaurant(Jiang Dian). At west, Fit City Restaurant(Yi Cheng Lou), Fourth Zhang's Restaurant(Yao Zhang Si Dian), Ban's Restaurant(Ban Dian). Near Gold Beam Bridge, there is Liu's Restaurant(Liu Lou). Near Cao Gate, Tryndamere Restaurant(Man Wang Jia), Cheese Zhang's Restaurant(Ru Lao Zhang Jia). At north, Eight Fairies Restaurant (Ba Xian Lou). Near Dai Building Gate, Eighth Zhang's Headquarter Restaurant(Zhang Ba Jia Yuan Zhai Zheng Dian). Near Zheng Gate, River Wang's Restaurant(He Wang Jia), Seventh Li's Headquarter Restaurant (Li Qi Jia Zheng Dian). Near East Imperial Ancestors Temple, there is Forever Celebration Restaurant(Chang Qing Lou). There are seventy two famous restaurants in the capital, I could not enumerate all of them here. The remaining ones are all small restaurants (Jiao Dian) which could not produce liquor by themselves, they have to buy from shops designated by Monopoly Bureau of Liquor.

If you want to buy fine dishes and host your guests in your own house, you will go to Bai's Shop(Bai Chu) first, Zhang Xiu's Shop at Safe Prefecture Alley (An Zhou Xiang) in west of the capital, Li Qing's Shop(Li Qing Jia) near Preserve Health Gate, Guo's Shop(Guo Chu) in East Prostitute Alley, Song's Shop at the back of Empress Zheng's house, Brick Li's Shop near Cao Gate, Dice Li's Shop and Fat Huang's shop near Assist State Buddhist Temple. There are a lot of shops near Nine Bridge Street(Jiu Qiao Men Jie Shi) area with waving tavern signs. Forever Celebration Restaurant near East Imperial Ancestors Temple is prosperous for selling dishes too.

Foods and Deserts

All cooks in a restaurant are called Master of Making Food and Measuring Liquor(Cha Fan Liang Jiu Bo Shi). The young waiters in a restaurant are called 'Uncle'(Da Bai). The women who work in a restaurant with their coiled hairs high in their heads are called 'Dregs'(Jun Zao), who will pour tea and liquor to persuade customers to drink more. Furthermore when ordinary people of the capital notice foppish young men have party in a restaurant, they would go forward to wait them attentively and carefully to buy liquors, foods or call prostitutes or do this or that for them, these people are called 'loafers'(Xian Han). Some would go forward to pour liquor or tea, sing for them and dedicate various deserts, spice and perfumes to them, when the party is over, they would get some tip, these people are called 'Errand Boys'(Si Bo). Prostitutes of lower class would come forward without being called, they would sing for the guests, the guests would give them some tip to send them away, they are called 'Prick Guests' (Zha Ke), also called 'Station Party' (Da Jiu Zuo). Some people would come to put drugs, fruits, radish down to the table without being asked, then they would get some money, these people are called ' Spread Around' 'Sa Zan'. Many restaurants allow such a kind of activity. Only Coal Zhang's Restaurant and Cheese Zhang's Restaurant near Prefecture Bridge don't allow such a kind of people entering their restaurants, neither they sell low quality liquor, they only sell preserved vegetables and top grade liquor.

So-called foods include soup cooked from various materials, thick porridge, quail soup, three crispy soup of bamboo shoot, mushroom and matrimony vine soup, mixed pork and chicken kidneys soup, mushroom with chicken soup, mixed stew soup, cold pea flour noodle, jade like knife cut slice noodle, fairies soup, cooked globefish, minced blanched vegetables, mandarin fish, turtle, pea flour skin stuffed with cassia leaves, cassia seed soup, pig intestine stuffed with vinegar seasoned ground pork, shark cooked in two ways, fish seasoned with basil, clam-like minced fish, fried pancake stuffed with ground pork and sealed with flour paste at the sides, griddle cake with sesame stuffed with ground pork, soup boiled with bones, milk like sheep meat with bone, boiled mutton, cooked mutton from butchered sheep on spot, roasted kidney, steamed duck and goose, kidney cut with lines like skin of lychee, fried kidney first blanched, roasted pork steak, fried pieces of duck meat coated with wheat flour, roasted bovine stomach, sauce basted sheep head, roasted whole sheep, roasted sheep head pieces, roasted goose and duck pieces, roasted chicken pieces, fried rabbit meat, fried rabbit meat with green onions, cooked fox meat, shredded intestine and stomach soup, intestine cooked with pebble stones inside, river deer meat with bone, fried quail, fried clam, fried crab, boiled crab, boiled crab with ten ingredients and spices etc., the dishes could be ordered on spot. If guests want to order extra dishes while they are having their food, the dishes will be prepared and served in a short while.

Outside of restaurant, some people would sell roasted chicken, stewed duck, cured sheep feet, sheep head meat, bovine large blood vessel, cured meat, shrimp with chopped ginger, crab cooked with liquor, cured river deer meat sliced in thickness like a chopstick, deer breast meat, deserts, seafood, seasonable fruit, sliced asparagus lettuce, lettuce, bamboo shoot from West Capital in plates. Some young men with white clothes and blue colored towel around their waist take a white porcelain pot to sell preserved spicy vegetables.

Some people would sell dried fruits such as ginkgo, chestnut, pear, pear slice, peeled pear, boiled jujube, stoned and skinned and baked green jujube, stoned and skinned and baked pear and peach, walnut kernel, teeth-like jujube, citrus, plum, crabapple, smoked plum, plum slice, boiled cherry, snow pear, birch-leave pear, phoenix pear, pear from Zheng County, pomegranate, papaya, hard pear, grape, lion-like sugar-white sesame mixture, bee-like rock candy, olive, tangerine, orange, cumquat, longan, lychee, lotus root, sugar cane, callery pear, dried crabapple, dried plum, longevity fruit, Chinese torreya, hazelnut, Chinese banana etc. Candied fruits, candied plum, candied pomegranate, chewing spicy ball(like chewing gum), small tea cake(baked tea powder, ground to fine powder, mixed with cooked rice, poured into a model, pounded solid with a mallet, then baked), borax pill etc. Restaurants also sell steamed mutton stuffed bun, minced pork or mutton ball, dried jerky, fermented fish, dried fish, cured fish etc.

Other small restaurants also sell various dishes such as fried fish, fried duck, fried rabbit, cooked pork preserved in fat, plum juice, cooked blood curd soup, lotus soup etc. Each portion costs 15 coins.

Each restaurant has a courtyard, covered passage way, and private rooms. Each private room has a suspension window with flowers and bamboos, at the entrance there is door curtain, prostitute would sing and guests could have fun in the room with privacy.

Volume Three

Clinics and Pharmacies in Horse Walk Avenue

You walk north along Horse Walk Avenue, you come to small shops, Time Restaurant(One of the 72 famous restaurants in the capital), Big Bequeath Orthopedic Pharmacy(Da Gu Chuan Yao Fu) till Old Feng State Gate. Along the avenue, there are many clinics and pharmacies opened by Royal Doctors with official violet uniforms and golden colored waist band, such as Gold Hook Jin(Gold hook is the sign hung up in the clinic), Cao's Unique Pill (for deaf and tinnitus), Landscape Painting Li's (for illness of throat and pharynx), Stone Fish Area Commander Ban's(Family name is Ban with ancestor once being an area commander, stone fish is the banner of the clinic), Silver Child Bai's Pediatric Clinic(Silver Child is the banner of the clinic),Big Shoe Ren's Obstetric (Big Shoe is the banner of the clinic). Others are shops for spice and perfumes and medicine, and the houses for officials. Night market is more boisterous than the one in Prefecture Bridge, the street would be filled with carriages and people in night, you even could not find a place to stand still for a while.

Streets and Alleys Out of Right Gate of Royal Palace

You go to west along the street in front of Declare Kindness Building, you will pass through Right Gate and Zoroastrian Temple(Xian Miao), you turn south at the first crossroad to walk till Great Rite Bridge. State Council is located at the west side of the avenue. From the east gate of State Council, you come the street of in front of State Council. At the south side of the street, you come to Bureau of Imperial Censor, you go west further along the street, you come to Temple Of Heaven And Earth(A place to sacrifice for Heaven in winter and Earth in summer); the south gate of State Council is across the back wall of Municipal Government of Capital; the alley in front of the west gate of State Council is called West Carriage Alley(Xi Che Zi Qu, in charge of royal carriages), Shi's Squash Soup Shop and Wan's Steamed Bun Shop are located in the alley. Qi Wu's(A famous general, strategist and politician lived in Warring Period 380 AD) temple is at the side.

You come out the alley, you come to West Turret Street at the southwest corner of Royal Palace. You come to a paved path, at the south side of the path, you come to the back gate of Peacefully Vitalize State Buddhist Temple(Tai Ping Xing Guo Si); at the north side, you come to Zen Enlighten Temple(Qi Sheng Yuan).

You go to west at West Turret Street, you come to Garrison Commander Center, along the street, you come to Cool Breeze Restaurant(Qing Feng Dian), Extraordinary Hotel(Wu Bi Ke Dian), WithFlower Zhang's Facial Cosmetics Shop(Zhang Dai Hua Xi Mian Yao), Royal Doctor Guo's Clinic (Guo Tai Cheng), Old Zhang's Pharmacy, Gold Turtle Pharmacy(Jin Gui Er), Ugly Grandma's Pharmacy(In order to solicit clients, owner would uglify himself or herself), Tang's Restaurant, till to Pillar Gate.

You come out of Pillar Gate, you go to west, at the north side of the street, you come to Build Prosperity Taoist Temple(Jian Long Guan), within the temple, a monk is selling drugs for dental disease, people in the capital all come to buy his drugs; at the south side of the street, you come to the mansion of Prime Minister Cai. You go further west, you come to West Entertainment Area(Zhou Xi Wa Zi) which starts at the north bank of Bian River from south, extends to north till Pillar Gate Street and merge with Inner Entertainment Area, the total length is more than 500 meters. You go further west, you come to former Fit City Restaurant(Yi Cheng Lou) at north side of the street. Further west, you come to Gold Beam Bridge Street and West Street, you come to Chaste Tree Twig Basket Pharmacy(Jing Kuang Er Yao Pu), Jujube Wang's Jewelry Shop. At the entrance of north alley, you come to West Branch Office of Prepared Medicine Monopoly Bureau (Shu Yao Hui Min Xi Ju). Further west, you come to Earthen Jar Market(Weng Zi Shi), an execution ground for Municipal Government of Capital. Further west, you come to Area Commander Gai's Pharmacy(Gai Fang Yu Yao Pu), Grand Buddhist Temple(Da Fo Si) and West Guest House of Capital(Du Ting Xi Yi), across street, you come to Weaponry Depot(Jing Cheng Shou Ju Suo). You go to north along a street at Earthen Jar Market, you come to Ban's Restaurant. You go further north along the street, you come to Big Three Bridges Area(Da San QIao Zi) and White Tiger Bridge, further north, you come to Wei Prefecture Gate.

Streets and Alleys at East of Prefecture Bridge In Front of Royal Palace

In front of Royal Palace, at east of Prefecture Bridge, near Bian River Street, you come to Assist State Buddhist Temple, the bridge is called Assist State Buddhist Temple Bridge, which is as level as Prefecture Bridge along Royal Street, further south, you come to Preserve Health Gate. At the west of the bridge, you come to Jia's Squash Porridge(Jia Jia Hu Geng), Sun's Excellent Steamed Bun(Sun Hao Shou Man Tou). Near Preserve Health Gate, you come to Pan's Astragalus Mongholicus Pill Shop(Pan Jia Huang Qi Yuan), Prolong Calm Temple(A temple for Taoist nuns, and nuns are from maids of palace, ordinary people are forbidden to visit). At the west side of the street, you come to Preserve Health Gate Entertainment Area(Bao Kang Men Wa Zi). You go east, there are a lot of hotels along the street along the inner city wall, officials from south, businessmen, junior officers all are staying in these hotels. Further east, you come to Avalokitesvara Temple(Si Shen Guan) and Socks Alley(Wa Yao Xiang). Further east, at the corner of the inner city wall, you come to Stabilize Force Temple(Ding Li Yuan), there is a portrait of First Emperor Wen Zhu of Hou Liang (907-923 AD).

You come out of Preserve Health Gate, you come to newly built Three Corpse Temple(They are responsible for reporting misdeeds of people to Jade Emperor at Geng Shen, Geng Shen is not a fixed date, for each calendar year, there are about seven such a kind of date, which varies depending upon the year. For example, in 2023, the date falls at Januaray 2, March 3, May 2, July 1, August 30, October 29 and December 28. Jade Emperor is the Supreme Deity of Taoism in heaven) and De An Gong Temple(A former minister of past dynasty). You go south to a bystreet going from east to west direction, you go to west along the bystreet, you come to Royal Street, the bystreet is called

Wheat Straw Alley. At the south of the alley, you come to the east gate of National University, then Water Tank Street(Shui Gui Jie), Yu's Dyeing Shop(Yu Jia Ran Dian). Further south, you come to Cloud Origin Temple(Fa Yun Si). There is another bystreet going from east to west, you come to Emperor's Son-in-Law Zhang's mansion. At the south side of Cloud Origin Temple, there is God Bless Taoist Temple(You Shen Guan).

Assist State Buddhist Temple Fair

Assist State Buddhist Temple Fair holds five times every month, people could come to the fair as they like. At the first gate, people sell birds, cats and dogs, you can find rare birds and animals in the place. Within the gate, you come to second and third gates of the temple, along the way and in the yards, people sell daily supplies. People set up colorful tents, stands to sell cattail mat , bamboo mat, screen, toiletry, saddle and bridle, bow and sword, seasonable fruits, cured meat and dried fruits. Near the main hall, Taoist Priest Wang's candied fruits, Elegant Character Zhao's(WenXiu Zhao) writing brush and Valley Pan's (Gu Pan) ink occupy fixed spots every time. Along the corridors nuns sell embroideries including laced long collar, flower, pearl ornament, head dress, colorful scarf, hat, hairpiece, hat for noblewoman, silk thread and band etc. In front of the highest hall Sage Aid Hall (Zi Shen Men) at the back of the temple, people sell books, curios and antiques, paintings and local produces from officials coming back from their posts to the capital, spices and perfumes. At the back corridor, there are people who are doing fortune telling, painting portraits of other people, selling methods for medicine, divination, and similar arts etc.

At the attics of the three gates and Sage Aid Hall, there are five hundreds bronze statues of Arhat, and Buddha's tooth remain is also kept in the temple. If people want to dedicate things to the Arhat and the tooth, the temple has to ask an imperial edict to allow to open the doors. There are a pair of glazed pagodas at each gate of the temple. There are Intelligence Sea(Zhi Hai), Benefit People (Hui Lin), Treasure Script (Bao Fan) , River Sand(He Sha), East and West Pagoda(Dong Xi Ta Yuan) courtyards, which are located at the back of the temple for monks. Each courtyard has its own monk official in charge of daily affairs. If the temple holds special mass gathering, it could prepare vegetarian foods, tea and fruits for 300-500 people in a short while.

Along the corridors of main hall, there are genuine wall paintings done by famous people of the dynasty: on the left wall there are Prajvalonisa Vjrabhairava Padvinasa-sri-dharani and stories about Buddha; on the right wall there is painting about Hariti is trying to eat his own child under the power of Buddha. There are also murals in the courtyard for sacrificed horses and musical instruments etc. The corridors are with elegantly and skillfully carved reliefs for people and grand palaces.

Streets and Alleys out of East Gate of Assist State Buddhist Temple

You come out of East Gate of Assist State Buddhist Temple, you come to a lot of shops selling man's scarf, waist band, books, hair dress. Ding's Vegetarian Restaurant is also located in the street. At the east side of the temple, you come to Prostitute Alley (Lu Shi Xiang), a lot of prostitutes live in the alley, and Embroidery Alley, a lot of nuns who are doing embroidery living in the alley. At the north side of the temple, you come to Little Sweet Water Alley(Xiao Tian Shui Xiang), there are a lot of restaurants selling southern style dishes and brothels in the alley. You go further north, you come to Celebration Li's (Qing Li)Preserved Ginger Shop. If you go north all way down along the street, you come to the street in front of east gate of East Imperial Ancestors Temple. You go further north then to east, you will come to Tax Bureau(Shui Wu) Street and Head Gao's Street(Gao Tou Jie). An alley at the back of Celebration Li's Preserved Ginger Shop is Painter Qu's Brother(Zhi Pi Hua Qu Ji Guan). In north and south alleys of Confucian Master, you will find Royal Doctor Sun's Clinic and a shop for boots. You will come to Song's Herbs Shop(Song Jia Sheng Yao Pu) at the entrance of North Alley of World Life (Jie Shen Bei Xiang), inside the shop at both walls you will see a lot of scenery paintings from Success Li(Cheng Li, a famous painter at that time).

You come out of the east gate of East Imperial Ancestors Temple, you go to east in the street across the gate, you come to former Bright Heaven Temple(Qian Ming Si), due to a fire accident, the place of the temple is occupied by Ritual Bureau(Tai Chang Si), Treasury Bureau(Tai Fu Si), Agriculture Bureau(Si Nong Si), High Court(Da Li Si), Royal Affairs Bureau(Zong Zheng Si), Construction Bureau(Jiang Zuo Jian), Logistic Bureau(Jun Qi Jian) and Education Bureau(Guo Zi Jian). You go further, you come to alley to south direction, the alley is called Third Sweet Water Alley(Di San Tiao Tian Shui Xiang). You go further east, you come to famous Bustling Hotel(Xi Xi Rang Rang Ke Dian) of the capital. You go further east, you come to HighSunshine Headquarter Restaurant(Gao Yang Zheng Dian) at the north side of the street, you will come to Horse Walk Street if you go north. You go further east, you come to Carriage House(Che Tu Yuan) at the north side of the street, you will come to Second Sweet Water Alley(Di Er Tian Shui Xiang) at south side of the street. You go further east, you come to Audit Bureau(Shen Ji Yuan). You go further east, you come to famous Han's Mansion in front of tung free(The family had two prime minister in the dynasty), you go further east to the front gate of Imperial Ancestor Temple. You go to south from the street in front of the gate, the alley is First Sweet Water Alley(Di Yi Tian Shui Xiang), from there you can go to Avalokitesvara Temple(Si Shen Guan). You go to north from the street in front of the front gate of Imperial Ancestor Temple, you will go to Elm Forest Alley which leads to Cao Gate Street, there are so many shops, restaurants and places along the way and nearby areas which would not be mentioned here.

Supreme Heaven Taoist Temple

Supreme Heaven Taoist Temple(Shang Qing Gong) is located at the north side of the street within New Song Gate, at the west side of the street is Cogongrass Hill Taoist Temple(Mao Shan Xia Yuan).

Mighty Spring Taoist Temple(Li Quan Guan) is located within East Water Gate.

Avalokitesvara Temple(Guan Yin Yuan) is located within Old Song Gate and at the south gate of Imperial Ancestor Temple.

Admire Virtue Buddhist Temple (Jin De Si) is at the back of Supreme Heaven Taoist Temple. There is Peach Flower Cave, prostitutes live in the cave.

Open Treasure Buddhist Temple(Kai Bao Si, one of the four largest Buddhist temples in the capital) is located at a byway outside Old Feng State Gate, there are twenty-four courtyards in the temple, Benevolent King Courtyard is the one most frequently visited by people.

Clear Sky Buddhist Temple(Tian Qing Si, one of the four largest Buddhist temples in the capital) is near Dim Light Bridge at the north side of the capital.

Prosper Virtue Buddhist Temple(Xing De Yuan) is located outside of Golden Water Gate.

Longevity Taoist Temple(Chang Sheng Gong) is located Lu's Alley.

Manifest Calmness Buddhist Temple(Xian Ning Si) is located at the north side of Coal Alley(Tan Chang Xiang).

Buddha Stage Temple(Po Tai Si) is within Chen Prefecture Gate.

Tusita Temple(Dou Sui Si) is located at Red Gate Alley in northwest direction of Old Feng State Gate.

Bodhisattva Surge Temple(Di Yong Fo Si) is located at the south side of Fodder Alley at the west of the capital.

Cleanse Karma Temple(Shi Fang Jin Yin Yuan) is located in Oil Vinegar Alley(You Cu Xiang) at the west of the capital.

Bathroom Buddhist Temple(Yu Shi Yuan) is located in Third Sweet Water Alley.

Alms Buddhist Temple(Fu Tian Yuan) is located outside of Old Cao Gate.

Requite Favour Buddhist Temple(Ba En Si) is located Royal Salt Alley.

Supreme Harmony Taoist Temple(Tai He Gong) is located at Grand Bridge Street at the west of the capital.

Profound Origin Taoist Nunnery (Dong Yuan Guan) is located at the north side of Ban's Restaurant.

Precious Jade Taoist Nunnery(Yao Hua Gong,for deposed imperial concubines only) is located outside of Gold Water Gate.

Long Live Taoist Temple(Wan Shou Guan) is located outside of Old Jujube Gate and in front of Ten Princes Palace(Shi Wang Gong).

Horse Walk Street Residential Houses and Shops

You go north along Horse Walk Street, outside of Old Feng State Gate, you come to Zoroastrian Temple Byway(Xian Miao Xie Jie) and North Side Entertainment Area (Zhou Bei Wa Zi) of the capital. At the street within New Feng Gate, you come to shops, residential houses and barracks of imperial guards at the sides of the street, the street extends forward for about 5 km to New Feng Gate. There are a lot of alleys and streets and courtyards in the area, everywhere you go you will see crowd gates and people, you will see tea houses, restaurants, art performing venues, food and drink stands. The stand owners usually prepare and sell foods on the spot. If you want to have northern style dishes, you should go to Fourth Li's Restaurant, Duan's Stewed Food, Shi Feng's Restaurant near Pan's Restaurant; if you want to have southern style dishes, you should to Jin's Restaurant near Assist State Buddhist Temple Bridge, and Zhou's Restaurant at Nine Curve Alley(Jiu Qu Zi), these restaurants are best ones.

Night Market ends around 1 am, around 5 o'clock in the morning, business begins to open again. If you go to some bustling place, the business is open for twenty four hours. Even in some remote and quiet places, you can also buy stuffed bun (Suan Xian), pancake with pork sirloin, mixed vegetable pancake, badge and fox meat, porridge of forsythia leaves with minced pork, sausage, candy and deserts etc. In cold winter night, there are always night market even in blizzard. There are thinly sliced pork, fermented soybean with ginger, cooked thin slices of meat, cooked sliced pig and sheep innards, cooked sheep blood mixed with wheat flour, roasted sweet or salty wheat flour small pieces, fried liver, clam, crab, walnut, malt sugar, birch-leave pear, pomegranate, hawthorn, hard pear, glutinous rice cake, rice dumpling and salty fermented soybean sauce etc. in night market. Around one o'clock in morning some business men would begin to sell tea as people in the capital begin to go back to their homes after official or private businesses.

Carting Business

The big cart in East Capital is called 'Peace Cart' due to the cart with two or four wheels could only be moved in nice weather condition, in rainy or snowy day, the cart just could not moved forward anyway. The cart has a cargo box without lid, the box is made of railing, the inside of the box is smooth. There are two poles stretching forward from the box, the poles are about 60-90 cm, coachman works between the poles with his whip and rope halter. There are about twenty mules or donkeys in two lines or five to seven oxen pulling in front of the cart. The wheels are as high as the box, there are a pair of wooden brakes at the back of the cart. In night there is a small bell hanging in the center of the cart, thus people would know the cart is coming when they hear the bell, thus cart in opposite direction could take precautionary measures. Two donkeys or mules are fastened at the back of the cart. When the cart is coming down through a precipitous downgrade road or bridge, another coachman would intimidate them to stop, thus slow down the cart. 'Peace' cart could carry goods of dozens hundreds kilos. For governmental institution they only use donkey to pull the cart as the cart is a bit smaller.

The next one is called 'Flat Head', which looks like 'Peace Cart' and is just a bit smaller. There are shafts stretching forward the wheels, an ox would stand in between the shafts with its yoke. The coachman would stand at the side with a rein. Restaurants would use 'Flat Head' to carry liquor barrel. The liquor barrel is long with a bung hole and a spigot. Each barrel could hold 50 kilos liquor, each barrel of liquor costs about one thousand and five hundred coins.

A cart like 'Flat Head' is used to carry women, the only differences are with a palm fiber hood, front and back railing doors and curtains.

A wheelbarrow is pulled and pushed by handles at front and back by a person, respectively, one person would help at each side, a donkey is pulling in front, it is called 'String Cart'. The wheel is at the middle of the cart and half of the wheel is above the cart, goods are put at the left and right sides of the cart, one has to make sure the goods are balanced at left and right sides. The cart is used to transport bamboo, timber, tile and stone(there are two short sticks under the shafts to support the cart when it is stopped). If the cart does not have front shafts, then it could only be pushed by one or two persons, the cart is used by people who are selling cakes and cake made of glutinous rice flour etc.

There is also a kind of two-wheels cart which could only be pulled by people, it is called 'Loafer Cart'. There is another cart which is used to carry huge stone or wood, it is called 'Silly Cart' (The cart looks like a sleigh with straight runners and front and back cross braces and legs) for saving people's efforts.

There are also pack camel, mule and donkey with leather or bamboo pack with square baskets to carry things. People use cloth bags to transport grains.

A String of Coins in The Capital

When people do business, an official string coins has seventy-seven coins(A string of coins is supposed to have one hundred coins), in capital market a string of coins has seventy-five coins; when people buy fish, pork and vegetable, a string of coins has seventy-two coins; when people do business transactions of gold and silver, a string of coins has seventy-four coins; when people buy pearls, hire maids or wet nurses, small fowls, a string of coins had sixty-eight. The exact number of coins for a string depends upon various businesses.

Hiring

If you want to hire waiters, chefs, handicraft men, servants, you have to go to headhunter of each profession to recommend for you. If you want to hire maids, you have to go through broker.

Fire Prevention

For every neighborhood(There are about one hundred thirty five neighborhoods in the capital), there is a patrol office every 500 meters for thief and fire, each office has five soldiers for patrolling and delivering official documents. These soldiers are also in charge of night patrol and arrest suspects. In high places there are brick watchtowers, there are people on duty at the watchtower for observing fire. Under the watchtower, there are buildings for officers and soldiers, there are more than one hundred soldiers stationing in the buildings. There are fire extinguishing instruments such as small and big pails, ladle, mop with a long handle and hemp mass at the head to dip water, axe and saw, ladder, fire fork, long rope, iron cat(a long handle with iron hook at its end, a string of iron rings is hanging down from the iron hook, at the end of the iron ring there is another iron hook) etc. Whenever and wherever there is a fire, cavalrymen will immediately report to commanders of fire stations, the commanders of infantry and cavalry and royal guard, and Municipal Government of Capital will take firefighters to extinguish the fire, it does not need ordinary people to help.

Early Activities at Dawn

Every morning around 3 to 5 o'clock, attendants of temples begin to knock iron plate or wooden fish(an instrument monks used to make sound when they pray) along street to announce the arrival of morning. They have their own areas to work for such a kind of activity. They will beg alms in daytime in the same area. People who will take morning session at Royal Court or do business early in morning will get up upon hearing the announcement.

The gates of the city will be open, drawbridges will be put down, markets begin to do business. For example in a squash porridge shop, there is a lad sitting at the door, he is called 'Extra Bone' as he usually would add porridge or other things such as boiled perfused lung or fried lung to his customers. Wine shops begin to sell wine for twenty coins per serving, at the same time they also sell porridge and breakfast and deserts, sometime they will sell medicated water to wash face, tea or herbal water.

For those shops selling pork or mutton, people would carry sheep or pig on a shoulder pole or pull sheep or pigs on a cart, they often buy in hundreds. There are markets for fruits outside of Rosefinch Gate and at west side of Prefecture Gate. Papers and painting are also sold in the places, the places are bustling with people. For flour, businessmen would put it into cloth bag, each bag would hold 7.5 kilos, for big one it would hold 22.5 to 37.5 kilos. Businessmen would transport the bagged flour into the city as soon as city gates are open, they would sell till daybreak. There are also some people selling foods and medicines to those officials who are going to take morning session in Royal Court along Royal Street from Prefecture Bridge to South Gate of Royal Palace, they would hawk with various tones and voices.

Peddlers

If one has horses, two peddlers would come everyday to provide prepared fodder; if one has dogs, a peddler would come to provide treacle residual; if one has cats, a peddler would come to provide food and small fishes.

If one wants to tinker a hole in a metal container, washes mirror, repairs a cracked porcelain container, repair and maintain daily articles, repair shoe soles, wash waist band, repair head scarf for man and headdress made of white ox horn, and prepare scented incense coil, one would have fixed shops to take care of. One also has a fixed shops to take care of door plaque and to print Buddha portraits to send out as an alms.

Some people would pick water for household, each person has a special area to take care of. Some people would do lacquering, make hairpins and earrings, cut firewood with a big axe, change the handle of fan, sell scented cake for burning or carrying around, and provide egg-shaped briquette. In summer people would come to wash woolen products and dredge a well. If you want to get something done, so long as you pay your attention to your surrounding, you will definitely find someone to get the thing done.

Some people who are released from Army Band due to age or poor health would beat drums or blow horns in street to attract children and women to come around to watch, then they would take the chance to sell candy to them, these people are called 'Plum Seller' or 'Street Player'.

Everyday in front of mansions of rich people, peddlers would come to sell mutton, head meat,intestine, kidney, stomach, quail, rabbit, fish, shrimp, depilated duck and chicken, clam, crab, cured meat, spices, fruits etc. Peddlers sometimes would use coin as a gambling device to bet with residents for hairpieces, comb, laced collar, cosmetics, clothes, daily articles, bronze or iron instruments, clothes chest, porcelain articles etc. Sometime peddlers would use above articles directly as a bet.

At back street or empty space, people build tiny houses, the houses stand back to back, people call this kind of place as a 'courtyard', ordinary people live in such a kind of place, they would go out everyday to sell a drink from steaming pears first, then boil the steamed pears with sugar and jujube and honey, the drink is called Steamed Pear Jujube; yellow soft cake; steamed bun and bean sprouts etc.

In spring, government would send people to dredge the ditches in the capital. When people get the silt out, they would put them in a pit, the pit is called 'silt basin', only after governmental official finish checking the pit with silt, people could cover the pit with soil. When people are dredging in dark night, they have to be extremely careful for not falling into the ditches.

Volume Four

Military Officer Recommendation Department

Military Officer Recommendation Department(in charge of recommending military officers to have face interview and martial arts demonstration for Emperor, and so do to other military army commanders when they return from battlefield) will have one day off every ten days, the department is responsible for training of guard of Royal Palace, wrestlers and staff fighters.

Army barracks: Internal guard of Royal Palace stations in the palace. The guard has Right and Left Companies with 77 and 76 soldiers to guard Emperor when Emperor goes out of the palace. Besides the internal guard, there are also other security personnel in the palace under different names such as Nei Dian Zhi (54 soldiers), San Yuan(64 soldiers), San Du Tou(54 soldiers), San Zhi Hui(64 soliders) and San Zhi (54 soldiers). There are 20 soldiers(Xi Yu Zhi) for training and raising the royal horses; there are also soldiers who take care of horses when Emperor goes out, military bands, soldiers who are using arrow and bow, soldiers who are using spears, soldiers who are using other weapons. Everyday their commanders would supervise their practice. When provinces recommend martial arts practitioners who want to join army, they would demonstrate their martial arts to Emperor and his minsters.

Besides internal guards mentioned above, there are also garrison army to guard the capital. There are four divisions with total forty thousands soldiers, the names of the four divisions are Natural Valor(Tian Wu), Guard Sun(Peng Ri), Guard Dragon(Long Wei) and Guard God(Shen Wei), they are also called Royal Four Regiments.

There are also cavalry regiments for total twenty five thousands cavalrymen. The names of the cavalry are: Speedy Cavalry(Xiao Qi), Cloud Cavalry(Yun Qi), Guard Emperor(Gong Shen), Fierce Dragon(Long Meng) and Dragon Cavalry(Long Qi).

There are also soldiers under direct control of Royal Palace Commander and Infantry Commander, each has ten thousands soldiers(Hu Yi); Royal Navy Commander(Hu Yi Shui Jun) for seventy five thousands soldiers; Declare Valor(Xuan Wu) for seventy five thousands soldiers; Mighty Valor(Shen Yong) and Great Valor(Guang Yong) each for five thousands soldiers; Flying Mountain(Fei Shan), Quick-firing Bow(Chuang Zi Nu), Mighty Hero(Xiong Wu) and Extreme Strength(Guang Gu) battalions.

There are also soldiers with names of Declare Loyalty(Xuan Xiao), Six Army(Liu Jun), Strict Army(Wu Xu), Harmonious Army(Wu He) and Street Maintenance (Jie Dao Si) to provide logistical service with several hundred soldiers each.

About five thousand soldiers are guarding other palaces, mansions, temples out of the royal palace for Emperor and his relatives.

There are also handicraft men in charge of repairing and maintenance of Royal Palace and Ancestor Worship Hall etc.(Xiu Nei Si); making wooden, leather, stone, brick, hemp, tile, bamboo, nail, fire powder, porcelain etc.(Ba Zuo Si); workshop for Extreme Strength Battalion(Guang Gu Zuo Fang); workshop of preparing daily necessities for Royal Palace(Hou Yuan Zuo Fang); Book Bureau in charge of writing materials and books(Shu Yi Ju); Embroidery house in charge of Emperor's clothes(Ling Jin Yuan); Elegant Embroidery House(Wen Xiu Yuan) ; Official Distillery Shop(Fa Jiu Ku) in charge of making liquors for Emperor, sacrifice and bestowing; Internal Distillery Shop(Nei Jiu Ku) in charge of making liquors for territorial states; Cattle and Sheep Department(Niu Yang Si) in charge of providing beef and mutton and other meats; Vinegar and Oil Depot;Imperial Carriage Department (Yi Luan Si) in charge of palanquin for sending Emperor to morning session, banquet, worship and sacrifice ceremonies, inspection tour etc.; Liquor and Tea Office(Han Lin Si); Shouters (He Tan) in charge of clearing way for Emperor when he goes out in a procession; Security Personnel (Wu Yan) in charge of clearing way for Emperor; Bearers of Palanquin(Nian Guan); Carriage House (Che Zi Yuan) in charge of carriages for Emperor, Empress, princes, and princesses; Internal Retinues in charge of keys, inspection, locking and unlocking palaces; Sacrifice Department (Shang Xia Guan) in charge of preparing materials for sacrifice ceremony; Yellow Uniform Servants (Huang Cheng Huang Zao Yuan Zi) in Royal Palace; Cleaners (Chu Chu) in charge of cleaning of Royal Palace. These people are under various departments.

Crown Prince Having An Imperial Concubine

When the crown prince gets married with his concubine, he has a full guard of honor with banners, umbrella, fans and weapons etc. When he has a banquet, he has a full military band. His concubine will take a carriage adorned with long feathers of pheasants, a round violet roof, curtains around four sides of the carriage, and jade strings hanging around four corners. The carriage is pulled by four horses.

A Princess's Marriage

When a princess gets married, she will also have guard of honor, curtain enclosure, walking screen in guarding against dust or obstructing peeping, and sprinkling water along way to guard against dust(When a prince or princes goes out, Street Maintenance would despatch dozens soldiers to clean and sprinkle water along way, it is called 'Shui Lu').

Several hundreds of 'Dan Chuang'(A long rectangular bed with side railings to carry on shoulders by two people with long poles) with dowries are carried soldiers of Natural Valor in violet uniforms with special head scarf. There are dozens of palace maids with pearl hairpins, silk hair ornaments, golden colored tasseled cape and other ornaments riding on horses in two lines around the palanquin. There is a cyan umbrella in front of the procession, it is called 'Short Tread'. There are people holding red silk fans with golden tassels walking in front and behind the palanquin.

Princess is sitting in a golden palanquin with palm fiber roof. The palanquin has red columns and ridge, on the roof there are copper cast cloud and phoenix patterns. The palanquin is about 1.65 meters in height, 2.5 meters in length and 1.2 meters in width. Six people could sit in the palanquin. There are bead curtains with embroidered tablets around the palanquin, the inner curtains are embroidered with white vines with flowers. There are railings around the palanquin with inlaid golden threads and engraved figurines and fairies. There are twelve people carrying the poles of the palanquin, there are green ribbons hanging down the poles from golden fish-like hooks.

Empress's Trip

When Empress Dowager or Empress has a trip, she still take a palanquin. The palanquin is wider than the princess's one. The engraved patterns on the palanquin are with dragons, the palanquin is with front and back palm eaves. The procession is similar to Emperor's but a few people. But the procession does not have the royal tablet(Jia Tou) handed down from First Emperor of the dynasty at the front of the procession and the security guards along the way.

When officials, wealthy and ordinary people have their sons or daughters get married, they still use palanquin without the bronze cast phoenix and flower patterns on the roof of the palanquin, the guard of honor at the sides of the palanquin could be hired. Also the clothes, caps and other things for the retinues could also be rented.

For ladies with an honorary title conferred by imperial mandate, dignitaries and ordinary people, they take a carriage looking like the palanquin used by the prince, and the carriage could take six people. There are railings in front and at the back of the carriage, the axle under the carriage and red wheels at its sides. The front shaft stretches forward for about two meters, and the carriage could be pulled forward by single ox. People could also rent the carriage.

Renting

When people have funeral service, there are funeral shops selling various things according to usual practice such as the leading paper figure in black overcoat and red skirts with gold eyes holding a dagger-axe and a shield (Fang Xiang), paper carriage, and other paper things for funeral. All the things have fixed price, thus the family need not to prepare by themselves.

If people go out for something, and the destination is a bit faraway, there are many places in streets and alleys around neighborhood to rent saddle and horse. It costs less than one hundred coins per service.

Routine Maintenance and Asking Monks

If one wants to repair house, or wants to have praying for dead ones in birthday or date of death by Buddhist or Taoist monks, they could go to market or the entrance of certain alley and street to hire workmen for doing wooden and tile works and other things. People will stay in the place to wait for being hired, these people is called 'Gather Place (Luo Zai)'. Bamboo and wood could be bought at special shops; so do the tiles and bricks.

Renting for Party

If ordinary people want to have party for a happy occasion or funeral, there are special shops to rent tables, chairs, plates, bowls, cups, chopsticks, layered compound square boxes for deserts etc.; there are also special shops to ask for chefs to cook for the party; there are also special shops to ask for host of the party, the person to send invitation cards, the person to arrange seats in the party, and the person to toast with guests in the party, these people are called 'Talkers' (Bai Xi Ren). All these people are called 'Four Errand-Men'(Si Si Ren, Four mean screen and dinnerware, cook, tea and liquor, and party host to put dishes on table and take care of guests).

If people want to have a party in a park, pavilion at lakeside, temple etc., they could hold at anytime and any place they like as there are many restaurants to offer the needed service. The service has fixed price according to normal practices, the people in charge of the service dare not to charge extra money. Even for party of a hundred people, the restaurant will get everything ready, satisfaction is guaranteed, the host needs only to pay the money and not to worry about anything else.

Meet Immortal Restaurant

For restaurants like Love Harmony Restaurant at east side of the capital and Meet Immortal Headquarter Restaurant within New Gate, often they are ready for a party about one hundred people in place, nothing would be allowed in short. As people in the capital like to be extravagant, thus they would always prepare extra things in hand. In a restaurant, even for two people in a table, they would prepare a set of wine ware for warming and pouring wine, two wine cups with a base plate, five plates each for cold dishes and hot dishes, three to five bowls for fresh vegetables, these dinner ware cost near one hundred silver taels(One tael silver cost about ten to fifteen hundred coins). Even only a person is drinking, the restaurant will serve him with silver Yu(a broad-mouthed receptacle for holding liquid). All vegetables, fruits and foods are very clean and elegant. If customer wants something else for their drinking, they would send people to buy for them for things like soft mutton, shrimp, crispy snails,steamed stuffed buns, salted fish, pickled cucumber with shredded ginger etc. from other places.

Restaurants

Big restaurant are called 'Share Tea (Fen Cha)', they provide thick porridge, stalactite soup(Shi Sui Geng, none is sure what kind of soup is it now), pork, pancake, soft mutton, spinal joints and big bones, stewed kidney, intestine cooked with pebble stones inside, roasted mutton, pita bread soaked in lamb soup, steamed cold noodle(Tong Pi Mian), hard noodle(Jiang Po Dao), thin and long noodle(Hui Dao), baked salty wheat flour pieces, braised string bean with noodle. If people order a full table, they will be given free vegetable soup.

There are Sichuan style restaurants for barbecued pork with noodles, braised noodle, noodle rinsed with cold water with thin slices of pork, fried then stewed pork, assorted cold dishes of entrails, cooked rice wrapped in lotus leaves. There are southern style restaurants for steamed bun with fish meat, steamed and braised cold noodle, rice with fried fishes.

There are squash porridge restaurants. In front of the restaurants there are decorated entrances with square wood and buntings, dozens of halves of pig and sheep are hung down on the square woods, the windows in the restaurants are decorated with red or green colors, they are called 'Welcome Gates' (Huan Men).

There are a courtyard, east and west corridors for every restaurant. When customers take seats, a waiter would come forward with a piece of paper and a pencil, ask every one around table for what they like to have. As people in the capital are extravagant, they would like to order various things such as hot dishes, cold dishes, whole piece, warm dishes, lean meat dishes, fat meat dishes, thus everyone has his likes. The waiter would take the order to the outside of the kitchen, begin to read for the chef, the chef is called 'Dang Tou'(Chef) or 'Zhuo An'. After the waiter finishes the reading, in a short while, a dish carrier would take dishes out with three dishes on his left hand, about twenty dishes layered up on his right arm from hand to shoulder. The waiter would pick up the dishes from the carrier, nothing is allowed to be wrong. Otherwise the guests could report to the owner, the owner would scold the waiter or the carrier, deduct their pay or even fire him on serious mistake.

When a customer enters a restaurant, they would be served with shallow glass bowl, the bowl is called 'Azure Bowl'(Bi Wan) or 'Zao Geng(Making Soup)'. With fine vegetables, it is called 'Making Fine'(Zao Ji), it costs ten coins per bowl. If meat is equal with noodle, it is called 'He Geng (Mixed Soup)'. If it is served for half a portion, it is called 'Dan Geng(Single Soup)'. In past people used spoons to eat, at the moment people all use chopsticks.

There are barbecued pork, special knife cut noodle(Bo Dao Mian, about 50 centimeters long per noodle), fried mutton, baked salty wheat flour pieces, wonton. There are also vegetarian restaurants for monks. There are also shaved noodle, vegetable noodle, hard noodle (about thirty centimeters in length and 2 centimeters in width), cake with fine fillings(Xi Gu Duo Er), rice served with meat and vegetable on top, rice wrapped in lotus leaves, preserved cucumber, radish etc.

Butcher's Shop

There are a lot of butcher's shops in the alleys, streets and markets in the capital. Each shop has three to five waiters to serve customer. Each shop sells raw and cooked meat. The meat could be thinly sliced, shredded or cut into pieces. In night, the shop would sell deep-fried meat or quick-fried meat. When a customer is buying meat, if the change is small, the seller would put some other meat to make the balance.

Pancake Shops

There are pancake shops selling fried dough cakes, some are selling sesame seed cake. For shops selling fried dough cakes, they also sell steamed buns, pancake filled with sugar, the pancakes could be put in a box or in a plate. For shops selling sesame seed cakes, they also sell pancakes brushed with oil just at the sides, deserts looks like chrysanthemum, horse-shoe like pancakes, deep fried cake looks like a sliding weight of a steelyard, pancake stuffed with bone marrows of animal, pancake covered with sesame seed and other styles. Three to five people are working as a group on a kitchen table, one is preparing dough, one is making it into various forms, one is putting into oven. From 5 o'clock in morning, one could hear the sound of kneading the dough on the table. Among the pancake shops, Zhang's Shop from Sea Prefecture in front of Great Grandfather's Temple and Zheng's Shop in front of Emperor's Residence(the living place before he became an emperor) are most famous. Each of the two shops has more than fifty ovens to bake the cakes.

Fish Shops

Fish shops use shallow pail (about one meters in length, thirty centimeters in depth, with 10 to 20 cm of water) to sell fish, the fishes will be isolated with willow leaves and kept in the pail. Peddlers also use the pail to sell fish along street and alley. Every morning, several thousands Dan(About sixty kilos per Dan) will go into the city through New Zheng Gate, West Water Gate and Victories Gate alone. In winter, fishes from Yellow River and other faraway places will be transported into the city with cart, the fishes are called 'Cart Fish', it costs less than one hundred coins per 640 g.

Volume Five

Folk Custom

All peddlers who sell food in the capital put their foods in clean containers, whether the containers are in cart or shoulder pole, they are all clean and lovely, people like them very much; as to the taste of the food and soup, they would prepare with their utmost care and seriousness. For those people who sell drugs or do fortune telling they also wear uniforms. Even beggars have to wear certain clothes according to the relevant custom, if they slacken a bit, they are not tolerated by people of the capital. Officials, scholars, peasants, handicraft men, businessmen and all professions, shops, restaurants have their clothes in comply with the characteristics of their profession, they dare not to violate a bit. For example a clerk working in spice and perfume shop has to wear a round cap and a shawl; a manager of a pawn shop has to wear black coat with short sleeves and a waist band with a horn as ornament without a round cap, etc. When one walks in street, based on his clothes, people would know his profession.

People in the capital advocate justice, if they see a person from other place is bullied by people of the capital, they would come forward to protect him. If someones are caught by patrol soldiers for fighting, they would step forward bravely to talk to soldiers on behalf of them, some would invite the soldiers to a restaurant and would face pressure from the office, but they would still come forward to offer their help. If an outsider comes to the capital and lives as their neighbor, they would lend him some utensils or help to buy some daily supplies, offer him tea, help him to find a place to establish his business etc. Furthermore, some people would carry a tea pot to deliver tea while delivering or sending messages among people. If a household is holding a party for marriage or birthday or funeral, neighbors would come to the household to help.

For those shops who are allowed to manufacture their own liquor with official licence, they dare to lend their silverware costing about three to five hundred taels to an owner of a small liquor who just comes to the shop two to three times. Even for poor people who come to the shop calling for sending liquor, the shop would deliver liquor in silverware. For those people who would drink for all night, the shop would send someone to take back their silverware in next day. For those brothels, the shop treat them in same fashion. It is so simple for those shops to lend their silverware, I think there is no other place like this in the world.

As the capital has so many people, if hundred thousand people come to the capital, people of the capital might not think there are more people in street; if hundred thousand people leave the capital, people of the capital might not think there are fewer people in street. The capital is really a place in which every place is filled with flowers, wine is stored in pool, spices is piled up like mountains, medicinal herbs is deposited like into seas. In remote street and narrow alleys, there are tens thousands restaurants for party and stages for dancing in the capital, I just don't want to bother to tell everyone of them to you.

Capital Theatre and Performance Center

SINCE 1102 AD, ALL theaters and performance centers in the capital are administered by Elder Zhang(TinSou Zhang, a famous artist) and ProudSong Men(ZiShu Men, an official in charge of performing arts).

For Xiao Chang(a singing form, a singer would hold clappers, sing slowly for poems written at the dynasty), the most famous ones include ShiShi Li(a famous singer and prostitute, Shi in Chinese character means teacher), PoXi Xu(PoXi is a common name used for famous prostitutes, sometimes man would use the name too. It means Mother-in-Law would cherish the girl in original meaning.), YiNu Feng(YiNu means it is proper to be a servant), SanSi Sun(SanSi means three four, usually it means when she was born, her mother was thirty four).

For Piao Chang(a variant form of Xiao Chang, a singer would beat a small drum, sing short song integrated with the mimic callings of peddlers with gaudy lyrics) Prostitutes: QiQi Zhang(QiQi means seven seven, which might mean some praise or evaluation about her), JingNu Wang(JingNu means capital servant), XiaoSi Zuo(XiaoSi means Little Fourth). Niang An(Niang means daughter, maybe Niang An means the daughter of An's family), Tuan Mao(Tuan means a mass, Mao means thread or hair if not used for Family Name) etc.

Royal Musician temporarily laid off: CuiGai Zhang(CuiGai means verdant cap, lid or cover), Cheng Zhang(Cheng means success). Their apprentices include: ZiDa Xue(ZiDa means elder Daughter), ZiXiao Xue(ZiXiao means younger daughter), Qiao Zi Er(Qiao Zi Er means a beautiful branch of a tree or flower), ZongXi Wang(ZongXi means always cherish), ShouNu Zhang(ShouNu means longevity servant), Cheng Xin(Cheng Xin means for your satisfaction) etc.

For short drama: Staff Head Puppet XiaoShan Ren(ThirdSon Ren,Staff Head Puppet(Zhang Tou Kui Lei) maybe is his nickname for playing puppet on his staff head) is very famous, he would perform at 5 o'clock in morning. If one comes late, one will miss his performance.

For marionette, GoldThread Zhang(JinXian Zhang) is famous; for fuse-propelled puppet(Ya Fa Kui Lei), OuterCalm Li(WaiNing Li) are famous. For jijitsu, wirewalking, acrobats skills, TrueWonder Zhang(ZhengMiao Zhang), ServantBrother Wen(NuGe Wen), SuperStrong(ZhenGeQiang),   NoBellyButton(Mo   Bo   Qi),

LittleDroppingKnife(Xiao Diao Dao) are famous. For somersault, hitting ball with stick, TrueAncestor Li(ZongZheng Li) and Brother Zheng(Ge Zhang) are famous.

For telling historical story, Width Sun(Kuan Sun), Fifteen Sun(ShiWu Sun), Alone Zeng(WuDang Zeng), Forgiveness Gao(Xu Gao), FilialPiety Li(XiaoXiang Li) are famous; for telling novel, Honesty Li(Zao Li), Independence Yang(ZhongLi Yang), Eleven Zhang(ShiYi Zheng), Brightness Xu(Ming Xu), ForeverProsperity Zhao(ShiHeng Xu), Nine Jia(Jiu Jia) are famous; for royal music, SmileFace Wang(YanXi Wang), RightTreasure Gai(ZhongBao Gai), FamousName Liu(MingGuang Liu); for tiptoe dancing, TrueServant Zhang(ZhenNu Zhang); for child wrestling, acrobats and broadsword hitting shield, GazeCapital Yang(WangJing Yang).

For shadow play, Fifteen Dong(ShiWu Dong), Seven Zhao(Qi Zhao), GuardHonor Cao(BaoYi Cao), Grandma Cao(PoEr Zhu), Sleepless Camel(Mo Kun Tuo), Windy Monk(Feng Seng Ge), SixthSister Zu(LiuJie Zu) are famous. For farce shadow play, Ceremony Ding(Yi Ding) and Lucky Skinny(Shou Ji) etc. are famous.

For small animals and fowl play, HundredFowls Liu(BaiQin Liu) is famous. For soliloquy and singing, ThirdGeneration Kong(SanChuan Kong) is famous. For riddle, Detail Ma(Xiang Mao), PrimeUgly Huo(BoChou Huo) are famous. For humorous talk, HillPerson Zhang(ShanRen Zhang) is famous.

For comedy, Fib Liu(Qiao Liu), NorthernMan(HeBeiZi), Success Bo(Sui Bo), LittleOx Wu(NiuEr Wu), FiveEyes Da(YanWu Da), BrightSuccess Chong(MingQiao Chong), LittleCamel(LuoTuoEr), Honesty Li(Dun Li) etc. are famous. For playing immortal and ghost, Third Sun is famous. For telling story about Third Kingdom Period(220-280 AD), Fourth Sun is famous. For telling story about Five Dynasty(907-979 AD), Principle Yin(Chang Yin) is famous. For imitating the calling of peddlers, EighthDaugther Wen is famous. There are also many people who are good at various shows, which could not be mentioned here.

Whether it is rainy or windy day, every house is filled with people everyday. The court musicians and military band would allow people to watch their performance when they take their one day off every ten days. When Royal Court is planning to hold a banquet, the office in charge of imperial music will call musicians together to practise one month before the scheduled date for dancing and music and acrobats and short play etc.

Betrothal and Marriage

The process of getting a daughter-in-law starts from exchanging drafts of basic information about the families(the basic information includes the address, essential information about what kind of officials the great-grandfather, grandfather and father were/are, the birth date(which is essential for determining whether the intended-to-be-couple could be matched by birth dates) of son-in-law(or daughter-in-law) and which order the son-in-law (or daughter-in-law) is in the family(for example first son or third son, or second daughter etc.), the official title of the mother if she has one, how many acres of crop field, how many rooms in the family, then the date). If both families think they could go further, they will exchange detailed information about the families and relatives(including information starting from their great great grandfather to the great grandson about officials, the croplands, what kind of officials had been etc.).

Then the future bridegroom family will send someone to carry 'Oral Approval Liquor'(Xu Kou Jiu) to the future bride's family. There is one bottle each in front and back basket, the bottle is wrapped with silk, adorned with eight colorful flowers and eight colorful silk ornaments or silver ornaments, the shoulder pole is wrapped with red silk, it is called 'Hand Over Red Pole'. The future bride-groom family will put two bottles of water, three to five live fishes, a pair of chopsticks back into the original bottles and send back to future bridegroom family, it is called 'Return Fish and Chopsticks'.

The next step is dependent upon the future bride-groom family. The family could directly send betrothal gift, or front money for formal betrothal gift, or relatives to future bride family to have a look about the girl. If the family wants to have a look about the girl, their relatives or future mother-in-law or her sisters to go to the girl's family. If they like the girl, they would insert a hairpin into her hairs, it is called 'Insert

Hairpin'(Chai Tou); if they don't like the girl, they would leave a piece of colorful satin(about 24 meters long) to calm the girl down, which means the marriage could not proceed further.

There are several classes of matchmaker(Every marriage has to go through a matchmaker): for first class she would wear scarf and shawl, would wear violet clothes (a kind of Chinese-style jacket with buttons down the front and stand-up collar without sleeves. The coat has slits under armpits and reach the knees), the first class matchmaker is responsible for matching official and royal families; for second class she would wear a cap, or wrap her head with a piece of square yellow cloth with a knot on her forehead or wear a skirt, she would take a blue parasol. The matchmakers always work in a pair.

When the marriage is settled with a betrothal gift, matchmakers would exchange information for the two families at first or fifteenth day of every month. When there is a holiday, the future bridegroom's family will send holiday season's gift, ornaments, mutton and liquor to the future bride's family. The future bride's family would return needlework of the future bride.

Then the future bridegroom's family would send betrothal gifts, then tell the future bride's family about marriage date, then hold the marriage ceremony.

One day before the wedding day, or in the morning of the day, the bridegroom's family will send ornamental crown and embroidered cape, cosmetics to bride's home, the bride's family will send return gift of official auspicious clothes and head scarf to the bride(Under normal circumstance, ordinary people could not wear official clothes, but when a person is having wedding ceremony, he is allowed to wear an official uniform for an official at the lowest rank). One day before wedding day, the bride's family will send people to prepare the bedroom for the couple, the bridegroom's family will provide bed, mat, desk and chair; the bride's family will provide mattress, bed clothes, felt, quilt, curtains, bed curtain and pillows, and set up dowries. The bridegroom's family will send gift money and liquor to these people.

In the wedding day, ceremony host will lead the bridegroom and the festooned carriage or palanquin to the house of bridegroom. The bride's family accept the people from the bridegroom's family, the bridegroom's family will send satin to urge the bride to finish her makeup, and let the musicians following them begin to play drum and blow suona horn to urge the bride to get into the palanquin. The people coming with bridegroom don't want to leave right away, they are shouting for gift money, it is called 'For Raising Palanquin'. After they get the gift money, they will carry palanquin forward. The host of the ceremony goes back first to the bridegroom's house, the people following the procession and the people at the side of bridegroom ask for gift money and gift, it is called 'Obstructing Gate'.

When the bride gets out of the palanquin or carriage, a geomancer will hold a dou, a measure for grain, with grains, broad beans, coins, candies, grass etc., sprinkle the content toward the gate while praying and chanting, children rush forward to pick up the beans and coins, it is called 'Sprinkling Grain and Beans', it is believed the things could repress the evil ghost of black sheep and ox.

When the bride gets out of the palanquin or carriage, she could not step on ground, and could only step on blue cloth strip or pelt. A man holding bronze mirror is walking backwards, leading bride to cross over a saddle, then a piece of grass and a steelyard, and cross the threshold of the gate, enter a room. In the room there is a screen hanging down from the center of the roof, the bride will sit in the center of the screen, it is called 'Sitting in Screen'(Zuo Xu Zhang), sometimes the bride could directly go to bedroom and sit in the bed, it is called 'Sitting in Fortune'.

Those who come into the room with the bride will drink three cups of wine, then retreat from the room at once, it is called 'Leave At Once'(Zou Song). All guests sit around dinner tables, after three cups, the bridegroom would put on auspicious clothes and a lot of ornaments on his head, he would sit on a chair in a long and narrow sitting bed within the main hall, it is called 'Sitting High'(Gao Zuo). First the matchmakers, then his aunts at mother's or father's side, finally his mother-in-law asking him to step down from the chair, then he would come down from the bed.

There is a piece of satin which is cutting into strips at its lower end hanging over the door horizontally of the bridegroom's room. When the bridegroom enters the room, people would rush forward to get a strip of the satin, it is called 'Luck Wrapping Door'(Li Shi Jiao Men Hong).

The bridegroom goes to the front of the bed to ask bride to get out of the bed, at the moment, each of the two families of the bride and bridegroom would take out a piece of satin, they would tie the two piece of satin together in a fashion of connecting rings , it is called 'Pulling Satin'(Qian Jin), the bridegroom puts the satin onto his tablet(a piece of tablet held before his breast when an official goes to be received by an emperor), the bride takes the satin into her hand. The bridegroom walk backwards, the bridegroom and the bride are looking at each other, they come to the ancestral temple to kowtow to the ancestors.

After the kowtow, the couple go back to the room, this time the bride walks backwards. When they get into the room, they begin to bow to each other. After the bow, they go to sit in bed. The bride sits facing left, the bridegroom sits facing right, women begin to sprinkle coins and colorful candies into the bed, it is called 'Sprinkle Screen'(Sa Zhang).

The bridegroom will cut from his left side and the bride will cut from her right side of their heads a bit of their hairs to tie together, then each of the two families will take out one bolt of satin, hairpin, wooden comb and hair ornament looks like a wheat ear as gift, it is called 'Knot Hairs Together'(He Ji).

Then the bridegroom and the bride each takes a cup which is festooned together with red silk, each puts the cup to other's mouth to drink, it is called 'Swapping Cups'(Jiao Bei). After they finish the cups, they would throw the cups with its festoon down under bed, if one cup is facing upward, the other cup is facing downward, it is called 'Extremely Lucky'(Da Ji), people would come forward to congratulate them.

Then the screen of the bed will be shut. For royal family, the bridegroom will be carried out of the room by his retinue, for ordinary family, the bridegroom will come out of the room by himself, bow to thanks his relatives and friends, then sit down again to drink.

In next day at five o'clock in the morning, the bride kowtows to a table with mirror and mirror stand, it is called 'Bride Kowtow'(Xin Fu Bai Tang), then she would bow to elder members of the family, relatives, hand each one with satin, shoes, pillows or other needlework, it is called 'Award Congratulation'(Shang He). The elders would return another bolt of satin to the bride, it is called 'Greet Congratulation'(Da He).

Bridegroom would go to bride's family, it is called 'Bow to Door'(Bai Men). If the bridegroom is rich, the bridegroom could go to bride's family next day after the wedding, it is called 'Bow to Door Again'(Fu Mian Bai Men). Otherwise, he could go to the family in third or seventh day after the wedding. The gifts sent to the family are similar to what the bride took to his family. After the dinner is over, the bride's family will send the bride back with other necessary things appropriate for the ceremony accompanied by musicians who would beat drums and play suona horns.

In third day after the wedding ceremony, the bride's family will send satin, an oil lamp filled with sesame oil and honey meaning oil in honey for harmonious relationship for the newly wed couple and steamed cake meaning for rising prosperity, people from the family of the bride would come to the bridegroom's family, it is called 'Comfort Daughter'(Yuan Nu).

In seventh day after the wedding ceremony, the bride's family will take her back to her parents' home, her parents would give her a lot of satin and various jewelry, it is called 'Wash Head'(Xi Tou).

One month after the wedding ceremony, there is another big banquet to celebrate, it is called 'Full Month'(Man Yue). From then on, the courtesy will become less and less.

Having a Baby

When she was pregnant for one full month, her parents would send a bunch of millet straw in a silver or bronze or painted basin at the first day of next month. The straw is wrapped with beautiful brocade or colorful cloth, flowers are inserted onto the straw, so are the figurines made of ricepaper pith with five boys and two girls. They will send steamed buns in a box to their daughter, it is called 'Sharing Pain'(Fen Tong). They will also prepare cakes in a form of sleeping sheep or crouching deer to mean 'Sleeping Down'(Mian Wo) and clothes and other things for newborn, it is called 'Urge Birth'(Cui Sheng).

When she gives birth of the baby, people would come to send millet, rice, coal and vinegar etc. as gifts.

Three days after the birth, umbilical cord will come off, moxibustion will be given to fontanel.

It is called 'One La'(Yi La).

When the baby is a full month old, the family will use colorful silk thread, cloth and coins, the rich will use gold, silver, rhinoceros horn, jade and other valuables to prepare for 'Bathing Baby Party'(Xi Er Hui). Relatives would take part in the party, they would prepare scented bath water, drop fruits, coins, green onion and garlic in the water, surround the bathing basin with dozen meters silk ribbon, then a hairpin to stir the scented water, it is called 'Stir Basin'(Jiao Pen). Relatives and friends would come forward to drop coins in the basin, it is called 'Add Basin'(Qian Pen). If jujubes are standing erectly in the water, women would rush forward to pick up to eat them, as it is a good sign for getting pregnant with a boy. After the bath, the baby will be shaved of his lanugo, the family will take the baby to thank their guests for coming to the party, then the baby will be taken to his aunt's room, it is called 'Transfer Room'(Yi Ke).

In one hundred day, the family will have another party, it is called 'One Hundred Years'(Bai Sui).

When the baby is one year old, it is called 'One Year'(Zhou Sui). There will be a ceremony to put things of food, fruit, imperial decree or official appointment, writing brush, book, abacus, balance, thread and other articles around the floor, let the baby choose and the adults will watch which thing the baby would pick up first, it gives a sign what the baby is good at in future, it is called "Test Year'(Shi Sui, the activity is still held in parts of China at moment). It is a big ceremony for the child.

Volume Six

January

January first, it is New Year. Municipal Government of Capital allow people to bet on things for three days. Officials and ordinary people congratulate each other, businessmen will use food, daily articles, fruits, cakes, firewood, coal etc. as a bet, they would chant and shout loudly to solicit people to come to make a bet. For example, in Horse Walk Street, Pan's Restaurant Street, outside of Song Gate at the east side of the capital, at the bystreet outside of Pillar Gate at the west side of the capital, outside Feng State Gate at the north side of the capital and at the south side of the capital, there are a lot of festooned tents spreading with hat, comb, a double-edged fine-toothed comb, pearl, jade, headwear, clothes, flowers, laced long collars, shoes, boots, antiques and treasures. There are also show booths among the tents. The places are filled with people and carriages. Women from the rich and the powerful also come to the places in evening to take part in the bet or go into show booths or enter restaurants to have a party to have fun for themselves, people do not laugh at and are not a bit surprised by the thing as they are just normal practices. People act in same fashion in three days for Tomb Sweeping Day and Winter Solstice Day, respectively.

January First Morning Session at Royal Court

In January first there will be a grand morning session at Royal Court. Emperor holds the grand morning session in Grand Celebration Hall. Four tall strong armored guards stand at the four corners of the hall, they are called 'Guard General'(Zhen Dian Jiang Jun). Envoys from various countries come to send their greetings. Full royal procession of ceremony including guard of honor are standing in courtyard, all officials wear their official uniforms with black gauze hat with two wings at the back.The people who have passed the imperial examination(Ju Ren) held at provincial level also come to take part in the session, they are allowed to wear an official uniform of white gown with blue lace and a cap with two ridges (Ordinary official uniform has only one ridge). Stationing Officers of various provinces in the capital will take part in the session with local produces as tributes.

Envoys include: The envoy of Great Khitan State(Da Liao, a country at the northeast of Song Dynasty) wears gold cap with its back brim looks like long pointed lotus leaves, violet close-fit gown, gold multi-functional waist band, and deputy envoy of Great Khitan State wears violet uniform looks like an ordinary uniform of the dynasty with gold waist band. When the envoy bows to Emperor, he would only kneel his right knee down to ground while putting his hands on his shoulders. The deputy envoy kneel down to Emperor like the officials of the dynasty. The envoys of Xia Guo(Xi Xia, a country at northwest of Song Dynasty) all wear gold caps, red close-fit clothes, gold waist band and pantyhose. Their caps are short and small. They would bow to Emperor while crossing their hands in front of their chest. Envoys of Korea and Southern State(The state covers a region of current Viet Nam) kneel down to Emperor like the officials of the dynasty. Envoys of Hui Qi (The state covers a region of current Outer Mongolia and Russia) have large noses and long beards, their head is wrapped a long cloth or silk, they throw on their clothes. Envoys of Yu Tian(The state covers a region in current Xinjiang region) wear small pelt cap and, golden gown with waist band. They come with their wives on camels with pelt packages and bronze bells. Envoys of San Fo Qi(The state covers a region of current Indonesia and Malaysia and Philippines) are thin and short, their heads are wrapped with cloth, their clothes are weaved with Buddha's pattern. Envoys of Five Southern Vassal States (The states covers a region in current Guangxi and Laos) wear black pelt cap and have their hairs coiled into a cone like form, they greet Emperor like monks bow to Buddha. After the greetings, Emperor will award them with Chinese brocade clothes. Sometimes Zhen La(a region covers current Cambodia, Thailand), Da Li(a regions covers current Yunnan Province) and Da Shi (a region covers current west part of Iran) would send envoys to pay tribute.

Envoys of Great Khitan State stay in Capital Guest House; envoys of Xia Guo stay in West Guest House; envoys of Korea stay in Tong Wen Guan(Same Character House, a place special for accepting people from Korea) in AnZhou(Safe Prefecture) Alley outside of Liang Gate; envoys of Hui Qi and Yu Tian stay in hotel of Department of Protocol. Envoys of vassal states stay in LookCloud House(Zhan Yun Guan) or RememberRemoteness Guest House(Hui Yuan Guan). Emperor sends officials to hold banquets only for envoys of Great Khitan State and Korea on his behalf in their hotels.

The envoys of Great Khitan State would burn incense and pray in Assist State Buddhist Temple in next day; in the day after next, the envoys would go to South Royal Garden to shoot arrows. The imperial court would send some officers who are good at shooting to accompany them, all the members of the envoy will take part in the activity, and Emperor will let officials hold a banquet for them on his behalf in the garden. Dozens of soldiers of Arrow Shooting Battalion would guard around the target for the archery. The envoy would shoot a crossbow. A soldier of his with a round cap and a brocade coat will pull the crossbow open, dance for a bit, put the arrow on the crossbow, hand the crossbow to the envoy. The solider has already aimed at the target, the envoy only needs to release the arrow. According to usual practice, the officers who accompanies the envoys would shoot with an ordinary bow. If he hits the target, he would be awarded with clothes adorned with gold and silver jewelry, silver saddle, clothes, gold and silver articles, the award is different each time. If the officer win the shooting game, young people of the capital would greet him with poems on their way back from the garden, there are so many people coming along the way, they would from a human wall and obstruct the way.

Next day, the envoys would say goodbye to Emperor. As soon as the morning session ends, many lanterns and decorations are immediately set up in front of Royal Palace, they do it so quickly as if they are assisted by deities.

Beginning of Spring

One day before Beginning of Spring(One of twenty four seasons in lunar calendar in China which symbolizes the beginning of spring), Municipal Government of Capital will send an ox to Royal Palace to whip the ox for announcing the beginning of spring to admonish people to pay attention to their plowing. KaiFeng(Grant Titles) and XiangFu(Lucky Symbol) counties under Municipal Government of Capital will have an ox in front each of their offices. The staffs of the counties would hold a ceremony like prefectures and counties in other places. At the sides of the office, people begin to sell small cattle, the cattle is put on colorful clothes and led into a place enclosed with colorful railings, there are figurines from various operas and acrobats on the railings. People exchange head wears such as hairpins with a string of small colorful pieces which looks like a banner and paper flowers to be inserted in heads of women in the day. In the day, prime ministers, princes and other senior officials would be awarded with golden or silver banner- like ornaments to be inserted onto heads by Emperor. After the ceremony in Royal Court, they would insert the banners on their heads and return to their homes.

Lantern Festival

January fifteenth is Lantern Festival.

In front of Royal Palace, Municipal Government of Capital has already begun to put up colorful tents, huge wooden poles erected are right across Declare Kindness Building since Winter Solstice. From then on visitors begin to show up in Royal Street, a lot of artists with extraordinary skills, singers and dancers begin to perform in the corridors along Royal Street. The sounds could be heard more than five kilometers away. There are various activities such as Ji Wan(a game like baseball), Cu Jiu(a game like football, a ball with a leather skin stuffed with millet bran), wire-walking, pole-climbing, jujitsu by WildMan Zhao(YeRen Zhang, who would bend his back backwards and eat cool noodle with his mouth), swallowing iron sword by NinthBrother Zhang(JiuGe Zhang), fuse-propelled puppet by OuterCalm Li(WaiNing Li), sprinkling five-colored waters by young people(Waters made from herbs which would produce different colors), mud ball magic on spot (mud ball prepared on the spot will turn to dry one at once in the magic), acrobats and comedy, two-string bowed instrument by BigHead Wen(DaTou Wen) and Little Cao(Xiao Cao), clarinet by Thousands Dang(Qian Sang), magic fire powder show by Fourth Sun, pagoda of bowls and kicks round stone disc etc by Twelve Wang(ShiEr Wang), farce by Meet Zou(Yu Zou) and Field Tian(Di Tian), professional football by Ten Su(Shi Su) and Announce Meng(Xuan Meng), story about Five Dynasty(907-979 AD) by Principle Yin(Chang Yin), small animals and fowl play by HundredFowls Liu(BaiQin Liu), drum and flute music by ElegantCharacter Yang(WenXiu Yang). There are also monkey shows, fish jumping out of gate of knives, butterflies dancing and calling ants out to play etc. There are also people who are selling drugs, doing fortune telling and writing characters on ground by sprinkling fine powder of sand or stone. There are new shows every day, you always would be surprised by what you are watching.

At January 7, envoys go to Royal Palace to say goodbyes to Emperor, then they come out of the palace, the lanterns and festooned tents and colorful banners are everywhere, everywhere is resplendent and magnificent with glittering things. Lanterns are hung up in northern direction facing Royal Palace with paintings about immortal tales or peddlers selling drugs or doing fortune-telling. There are three festooned gates at the north end of the show, there is a placard at the top of each gate with characters written with golden ink: the middle gate is called Capital Gate Passageway(Du Men Dao); the right and left ones are called Right and Left Guard Gates(Zuo Young Jin Wei Zhi Men). The placard is with characters 'Emperor Shares Happiness with His People'(Xuan He Yu Min Tong Le). At the left and right sides of the gates, there are the images of Bodhisattva Manjusri on a lion and Samantabhadra Bodhisattva on a white elephant made of colored ribbons, respectively, there are five water columns coming down from their five fingers, and their hands are waving continually. Water is hoisted into wooden tank at high place by pulley, the water will come down like waterfall regularly. There are two frolic dragons made of straws and covered with blue cloth on the tops of left and right gates. There are tens thousands lighted lamps placed on the dragons, when one looks from faraway, the dragons look like roaming undulating dragons.

From the gates to Declare Kindness Building, there are more than three hundred meters distance, the space is enclosed with thistles and thorns, it is called 'Thistle Basin'(Ji Pen). In the center there are two erected wooden columns dozens meters high, there are colorful banners of silk and paper with paintings of immortal and other legendary figures at the top, the banners are waving in wind, it seems the fairies walking in air. There are music tents in the 'Thistle Basin' , royal bands and military acrobats are playing music and acrobats in the tents under a single commander.

There are yellow screens everywhere on the top of Declare Kindness Building. In the center there is a seat for Emperor, there are yellow tent around the seat, the guards of honor hold yellow umbrella and big fans(a big fan with a long handle, used in parades) outside of the tent. At the two side buildings of Declare Kindness Building, a huge balloon is hung on each building, the diameter of the balloon is more than 3 meters, there is lighted huge candle within the balloon. There is also music playing in the tent, the giggling sound of empress and concubines could be heard by people down the building at the foot of the wall of Royal Palace.

At the foot of Declare Kindness Building, there is a temporary stage constructed by wood, the stage is festooned with colored ribbons around its railings. At the sides of the stage there are guards with brocade uniforms, scarves with hairpins awarded by Emperor, long rods with their heads wrapped with iron balls facing the stage. Royal bands, military bands and ordinary performers are playing short plays. The royal guards are standing at the entrance of the stage. People are watching the show under the stage, the musicians are leading the audiences to shout 'Long Live Emperor' from time to time.

Emperor Visit Wu Yue Temple on January 14th

On January 14th , Emperor goes to visit GreetLuck Pond(Ying Xiang Chi) of Wu Yue Temple. There will be a banquet holding for his officials in the temple. Emperor returns to the palace late in night.

His personal guards wear big hats with ball-like ornaments and ornamental flowers, red brocade uniforms, and golden waist bands, and hold long rods with their heads wrapped with iron in different forms. The soldiers of Natural Valor wear scarves with the ends of the scarf bending upwards, with violet uniforms without sleeves and swan-like silk buttons. The soldiers of Right and Left Companies wear scarves with the ends of the scarf bending backwards, uniforms braided from scarlet, blue and violet threads, ride on horses with swords and bows and saddles of same pattern, hold a horsetail whisk to lead the procession. Guards of honor wear scarves with one end of the scarf pointing toward sky and the other end of the scarf coiled, red uniforms with two squares overlapped pattern, and broad waist bands. They take the articles for Emperor such as golden folding chair, spittoon, water pot, fruit plates, big fans, horsetail whisk etc. Emperor's chair and backrest are lined with yellow brocade and adorned with pearls along the edges and carried by his personal guards. Other guards also wear scarves, brocade uniforms with waist bands.

Usually when Emperor goes out, there are two hundred pairs of red silk lanterns with golden ornaments, in Lantern Festival, there are glass lanterns with long handles and ornamental jades added to the procession. Royal couriers hold red silk lantern with ornamental jades. When the procession of Emperor approaches, the security personnel form several lines. There is a person holding a crescent-like small stool covered with brocade on a horse back, dozens of Natural Valor surrounds the man and horse, whiling shouting: 'Attention! Emperor is coming!". They are followed by hundreds of junior officials of Ministry of Personnel with official uniforms and pearls adorned rods on horse. His personal attendants and other officials wear violet, red and green uniforms. The commanders of Royal Palace Guards, infantry and cavalry, defense ministers and other officers are riding in front of the emperor as front guard. The sides are guarded by Royal Guards. The guards are strong and tall soldiers who are constantly watching the outside of the procession, if anyone dares to shout loudly, he would be beaten by the guards till blood is coming out of his body. The royal musicians and military band are performing in front of Emperor, Emperor is followed by other bands on horse to perform music. Outside of the guards at the back of Emperor are followed at the left row by prime minister and ministers and advisers, at the right row by princes and relatives of Emperor, the relatives are called 'South Officer' at the royal court as they always stand at the south part of the morning session.

When Emperor comes near, the guards would stand in several horizontal lines and whip to intensify the tense atmosphere. Emperor is followed by a red umbrella with a curved handle which is held by a personal guard on a horse. When Emperor enters the area of the lanterns, the soldiers of Imperial Carriage Department shout 'Emperor is coming', the procession will go around the area while walking backwards in dance-like fashion, it is called 'Pigeon Hovers'(E Xuan), the officer of Imperial Carriage Department will get reward from Emperor for his performance. Then Emperor goes to top of Declare Kindness Building, people will come to the sides of the performing stage under the building to watch performance.

January Fifteenth Emperor Goes to Supreme Heaven Taoist Temple

On January fifteenth Emperor goes to Supreme Heaven Taoist Temple, Emperor holds a banquet for his ministers in the temple. Emperor returns to Royal Palace in evening.

January 16th

January 16th, Emperor does not go out. After his breakfast, he would come to the top of Declare Kindness Building, while music is playing, door curtain is pulling up, Emperor sits at the side of the balustrade to see common people. For those people who come to the downstairs of the building could look up to see Emperor: Emperor wears a small cap and red gown and sits at the side of a small table. His personal attendants are standing at his sides, other attendants hold umbrellas and big fans outside of the door curtain. In a short while, the curtain is dropping down, the music begins to play again, people could watch plays and activities as they like.

At the two side buildings of Declare Kindness Buildings: At the left building are the tents of Prince Yun and other princes; at the right buildings are the tents of Prime Minsters and Ministers and relatives of Emperor. From time to time, a flying pigeon(a pigeon-like box goes down through rope to the side buildings) would fly down to the side buildings for a reward from Emperor to various tents. From these tents, the family singers sing new songs one after another, the sounds intermingle with the ones from the temporary stage at the foot of Declare Kindness Building and the tents in Thistle Basin and along the corridors, everywhere is filled with music and song.

Under the west side building, Municipal Government of Capital send soldiers to guard, the tents stand next to one another, criminals stand in front of the tents, from time to time, the criminals are sentenced and taken away, in such fashion the government wants to warn the benighted. From time to time, imperial instruction is passing down to the tents to pardon certain criminals. At the moment, big candles are lighted in lanterns, the lantern lights are against the bright moonlight, harmonious and auspicious atmosphere is filled in air, waving candle lights are intermingled together in misty air.

Around midnight, a red gauze lantern is pulling up and suspending in air, people of the capital know Emperor has returned to his palace. In a short while, whipping sounds are coming out from the downstairs of Declare Kindness Building, then all candle lights of dozens of thousands of the lanterns go out at once. Then carriages of the noble and the powerful come out of the front of Royal Palace, drove southward to Assist State Buddhist Temple one after another.

Tents are set up in front of the temple, military bands are playing music in the tents. In the corridors at the sides of the temple, there are lanterns with poems such as: *Milk way wants to come down from azure sky, bright moonlight immerses on stage like water*; *Trees shine colorful lights everywhere, bridges open for people in all directions* etc. The lanterns are made of wooden planks, the planks are engraved with characters, the lanterns are covered with silk with lighted candles, the lanterns are hung there one after another, people could look and appreciate them. The relic of tooth of Buddha is enshrined and worshiped in front of Sage Aid Hall, lanterns are floating on the surface of the pool in front of the hall, the noble and the powerful occupy the seats in front of the hall too. The most boisterous places in the temple are: Mother with Nine Children Hall(A mother is holding a child in her arms and four children each at her sides as a god of fertility), Intelligence Sea, Benefit People, Treasure Script, East and West Pagoda courtyards. Various colorful lanterns are set up in these places too, people are bustling around to watch the lanterns till daybreak.

All other temples are open for common people to burn incenses. For example Open Treasure Buddhist Temple, Admire Virtue Buddhist

Temple, Grand Buddhist Temple etc., all these temples set up music tents to play music and light lanterns. Only the royal temples don't have lighted lanterns. Preserve Genuineness Taoist Temple is famous for its jade column and jade curtain lanterns.

Streets and alleys of the capital: The spice and perfume shops, tea houses, liquor shops in Horse Walk Street all hang their own unique lanterns, the lanterns of the spice and perfume shop of Lotus Wang is particularly conspicuous, they also invite monks of Buddhist and Taoist to pray in front of the shop, the monks play cymbals in a fancy style and drums with three to four drumsticks, passing-by visitors would stop to watch the performance. At every gate of the city there is a musical tent set up by the municipal government. The tens thousands streets and alleys of the city are filled with lively shows. At the entrance of an alley without a music tent there will be a tent for shadow play, thus children could watch the play, and the adults could find their children in the place to prevent their children to get lost.

The royal guards station within Right Gate of Royal Palace, the guards set up a musical tent across the gate, allow their relatives to climb on the palace wall to watch lanterns. Emperor would reward them with tea, liquor and money for makeup. All the guards are not allowed to go out the palace to watch the lanterns, they would hang up lanterns with bamboo poles in front of their barracks, the lanterns are hanging in air, when one looks from faraway, one could see waving lanterns high and low, faraway and close in wind like shooting stars in night.

The gates of the city are all open in the festival. Within the remote alleys of the city, bead curtains and embroidered placard are hanging at the gates, prostitutes are showing up with elegant makeup and carefully drawn eyebrows, they are competing for their beautiful looks. Lustrous desire is helped by liquor, elegant gathering and happy meeting make everyone cherish each passing second, what a wonderful and prosperous night. Without awareness, it is deep in night. Expensive horses are galloping in streets, luxurious carriages are wheeling down streets, the streets are filled with the singing young men of the noble and the rich of the capital; music is coming out of tens thousands household for all night.

Businessmen sell plum, moth, bee, willow, linden leave-like headdress of white paper, women would insert the headdress on their hairs, also people wear white clothes in the night too. Businessmen also sell rice dumpling and burnt pancake. It is particularly needed to be mentioned about burnt pancake, when a businessman sells the pancake, he would put up a blue umbrella on bamboo shelf, the umbrella is adorned with many plum color little lanterns with golden laces, lanterns are also hung at the front and the back of the shelf, he would walk around the shelf on drumbeat, it is called 'Whirling Around'(Da Xuan Luo), the scene could be seen in many alleys and streets.

All the city gates are open till the end of Lantern Festival in January 18th. Sometimes the festival will extend by an imperial order, so are the gates.

Between 1119-1125 AD, from December on, lanterns will be hung on Old Jujube Gate like the ones hung on Declare Kindness Building in Lantern Festival, a temporary stage is also set up at the gate for performance. Old Jujube Gate is called Revere Dragon Gate officially. If you go to south till Treasured Registers Temple, you will see people are playing GuanPu(it is a game played with six coins, the coins are dropped onto ground, the win or loss of a game is determined by the number of heads or tails, the bet is usually daily articles such as clothes, food etc.)and selling things along the way. Outside of Morning Glow Gate, a watch stage is set up with thistles at front, the perimeter is about 60-80 meters. Businessmen who are selling dumplings, burnt pancake, sausage, a cold jelly of minced fish and pork, starch noodle, chestnut fried on spot, ginkgo seed, fermented soybean soup with deep-fried finger-like dough stick and meat, chicken, cumquat, olive, longan, lychee etc. come to the stage and are waiting for providing foods and fruits to Emperor. Emperor sometimes will stay within the stage, then the officials guarding gates, doctors, personal attendants and the commanders of Royal Guard would stand in front of the curtain, three to five musicians are playing music for him. Sesame cake is burning brightly in a basin, it looks like in day. For some ladies of officials who come to watch lanterns, the personal attendant of Emperor would invite them to drink from a gold cup, then order them to retreat. The activity continues till Lantern Festival, it is called 'Advance Reward'(Yu Shang). What particularly needs to be mentioned is Special Chef Zhou's squash porridge, he would sell one portion for 120 coins for the remain porridge after serving Emperor, it is really different with the one sold for ten coins in ordinary restaurants.

End of Lantern Festival, Exploring Spring of People of The Capital Out of The City

After Lantern Festival, people of the capital go out of the city to explore spring one after another.

At south side of the capital, there are Jade Ford Garden(Yu Jing Yuan, South Royal Garden), pavilions and ponds of Prep Schools of National University(Wai Xue) and Jade Immortal Taoist Temple(Yu Xian Guan). If you go west through Dragon Turn Bend(Zhuan Long Wan), you will come to Three Meters Buddhist Garden, Mansion of Defense Minister Wang(TaiWei Wang Yuan), Mansion of Head OriginalView Wang(JingChu Wang) in front of Confucius Temple. At Two Kilometers Bridge there is a small hill called Looking Ox Hill(Wang Niu Gang). If you go east through Dragon Turn Bend, outside Chen Prefecture Gates, there are a lot of parks and mansions.

At east side of the capital, outside of Song Gate, there are Merry Forest(Kuai Huo Lin), Water Chestnut Pond(Bi Qi Bei), Lonely Happiness Hill(Du Le Gang), Inkstone Place(Yan Tai, a burial place for a famous politician Yi Zhang, died at 309 BC),Spider Building(Zhi Zhu Lou) and Mai's Garden(Mai Jia Yuan). Outside of Rainbow Bridge, there is Wang's Garden. Between Cao and Song Gates, there are East Royal Garden(Dong Yu Yuan), Nunneries Bright Heaven Temple(Qian Ming Si) and Worship Xia Temple(Chong Xia Si).

At north side of the capital, there is Emperor's Son-in-Law Li's Garden.

At west side, you go to west along the street outside of New Zheng gate, and reach nunnery west of Gold Bright Lake. There are a lot of brothels in front of the nunnery. Further west, you come to Guesthouse, there are pavilions, stages, corridors, ponds, swings and merry boats in the guesthouse. Guests could rent the boat and hold party in the boat. Across the guesthouse, there is Lucky Bless Taoist Temple(Xiang Qi

Guan), you go further west, you come to Plank Bridge(Ban Qiao), there are Virtuous Men Guesthouse and Lotus Guesthouse, which are temporal staying places for officials going to work in River East(He Dong) and Five Special Prefectures of Shannxi(Shannxi Wu Lu). People usually hold farewell party in the houses. You go through Plank Bridge, you come to Lower Pine Garden(Xia Song Yuan), Primer Minister Wang's Garden(Wang Tai Zai Yuan) and Apricot Flower Hill(Xing Hua Gang). You go to south at the corner of Gold Bright Lake, you will come to Navy Alley(Shui Hu Yi Xiang), you could play at West Mill(Shui Mo), and Prime Minister Cai's Garden is there too. You go south from Gold Bright Lake, there is Avatamsaka Nunnery(Hua Yan Ni Si) and Younger Aunt Wang's Liquor Shop(Wang XiaoGu Jiu Dian) with Horse Wash Alley(Xi Ma Xiang). You go to north from Gold Bright Lake, you will come to Gold Water River, there are Liang Zhe(An administrative area including part of current Zhejiang and Jiangsu Provinces) Nunnery, Ba Lou Buddhist Temple(Ba Lou Si) and Horticultural Garden, there are various flowers and trees for different seasons in the place, and it is worthwhile to visit. You go south from Horticultural Garden, you come to Pharmacist Liang's Garden(Yao Liang Yuan) and Prime Minister Tong's Garden(Tong Tai Shi Yuan). You go further south, you come to Iron Buddha Temple(Tie Fo Si), Grand Bless Buddhist Temple(Hong Fu SI), and East and West Cypress and Elm Villages(Dong Xi Bai Yu Cong).

At the north side of the capital, you come to Admire Heaven Slope(Mo Tian Po) and Corner Bridge and Temple of Warehouse King(Cang Wang Miao), White Pagoda Temple(Shi Ba Shou Ni Si) and Fourth Elder Meng's Liquor Shop(Meng Si Wen Jiu Dian).

At the northwest of the capital, there is a Common Person Garden(a garden belonged to a former prince who was demoted to a common person(Shu Ren)), there are stages, pavilions, and wine cup flowing ditch in the garden. Visitors are allowed to go into the garden to enjoy spring.

Around the capital, there are a lot of horticultural gardens. Within 50 km, there are no empty fields around the capital. Gradually spring shows up in one garden after another with warm sun and clear sky. Flowers are competing to come out of white walls, waving green willows cover countryside roads. Luxurious carriage are wheeling down through warm roads, green grasses and booming flowers cover everywhere like green soft quilt. Gallant horses are neighing merrily, blooming apricot flowers look like colorful brocade. Yellow warblers are chirping among green and flowering trees, swallows are flying in clear sky. Beautiful women are playing music on pavilions at waterside, young scholars are singing while walking on an engraved and painted bridge with water flowing under. Everywhere when you look, you will find beautiful girls are smiling and laughing on swings; everywhere you go, you will find adolescent boys running and playing on green football ground. You explore to find rare flowers, you choose to find a unique spot to appreciate a beautiful scenery, from time to time a falling flower petal will drop into your golden wine cup; you will pick up a flower branch, you will insert red flower onto your hairs, roaming bees and dancing butterflies follow gallant horses returning homes quietly. Thus, Tomb Sweeping Day arrives.

Volume Seven

Tomb Sweeping Day

One hundred and five days after winter solstice, it is Cold Food Day. One day before cold day it is called 'Prepared Cooked Food'(Cui Shu) (as it is prohibited to use fire in Cold Food Day). People would use dough paste and jujube to steam a food looks like a flying swallow(Zao Ke), the swallows would be stringed together with a willow branch, the string will be inserted in lintel, it is called 'Zi Tui Swallow'(Zi Tui Yan, ZiTui Jie was a minister of Jin state of current Shanxi Province, he fled to a hill, the king of the state wanted him to come down to serve the state, he refused and the king set a fire on the hill, and he was burnt to death. Thus in order to honor him, people forbid to use firewood in the day). In the day girls older than fifteen would coil her hairs up in her head with a hairpin to symbolize that she is already a grown-up.

Tomb Sweeping Day is at third day after Cold Food Day. New tomb would be swept in the day by cleaning weeds, then dedicated with sacrifices. People of the capital will go out to suburb in the day. Half a month before Tomb Sweeping Day the palace will send people to take carriages to pay homage to imperial mausoleums. Relatives of Royal Family will be assigned to go to various imperial mausoleums and tombs to sweep and pay homages. Their attendants all wear violet clothes and white triangle scarf and blue puttee(all the clothes are provided by the palace). In Tomb Sweeping Day, the palace will send people to take carriages to Imperial Ancestor Temple and other Taoist temples to offer sacrifices to ancestors and died concubines. All imperial carriages are decorated with gold and copper, azure blue curtains, pearl adorned door curtain, big fans are held at the sides of the carriages, guards with gauze lanterns are leading in front of the procession, scholars and common people would stop to watch the procession in street. Shops for burning paper horses and other paper materials in the capital would set up the paper things like a tower in front of their shops.

The suburbs of the capital like bustling market, people who come out for tomb sweeping or outing are staying under trees or within parks with plates and bowls filled with foods, they are toasting with each other. Musicians and dancers of the capital spread among the parks and gardens. People go back to the city in evening with Zao Ke, steamed bun, clay figurines, toy broad sword, clay pavilions and toys, chess, painted and etched eggs etc., these playthings are called 'Local Produce Gifts Outside'(Men Wai Zhi Yi). The palanquins are adorned with willow branches and colorful flowers on the top of the palanquins and hanging down around. The palanquins are covered with these ornamental branches. From Cold Food Day on, people of the capital would go out to do tomb sweeping for three days, but Tomb Sweeping Day is the most bustling day.

During the festival, shops would sell thick porridge made of barley flour and powered almond(Chou Xing), barley cake (which is made of cold thick porridge which is cut into slices, then is eaten with molasses), cheese and milk cake.

People enter the gates of the capital slowly within setting glowing on willow trees along the moats; people enter their courtyards in half-drunkenness under bright moonlight with blooming white pear flowers. Soldiers stationing in the capital would ride on their horses and go out the capital in rows with military bands for outing in spring, it is called 'Swinging Feet'(Shuai Jiao). The army are with bright and fresh ensigns and banners, majestic military appearances, strong and sturdy soldiers and horses, that is another scenery for the holiday.

March 1st Emperor's Trip to Gold Bright Lake and Valuable Royal Garden

March 1st, outside Obeying Heaven Gate, Gold Bright Lake and Valuable Royal Garden(Qiong Ling Yuan) are open for ordinary people. Everyday before the date they would hold ritual practices to host Emperor's trip. Even Emperor's advisers, scholars and common people are allowed to watch the practices as they like, Emperor gives a clear order to forbid Censorate to file any complaint against any violation of any official in the period. The lake is at the north side of the street outside of Obeying Heaven Gate, the perimeter is about 5 km, the widest part of the lake is about 3.5 km.

When you enter the garden, you go west for 500 meters, you come to a hall at the side of lake facing northward, it is called Waterside Hall(Lin Shui Dian). Emperor stays in the hall to watch competition in the lake and hold a banquet for his ministers. Before the place was enclosed off with screens, after 1111 AD, it is replaced with a brick and wooden building.

You go further west from the hall, there is an immortal bridge which connects the south bank to the island in the center of the lake. The bridge has three arches with red balustrades and stone columns to support the bridges. The bridge arches up in the center, thus it is called "Camel Rainbow' as when one looks from faraway, it looks like a rainbow. At the north end of the bridge there are five halls at the center of the lake. The halls stand onto the stone stage as a foundation, the halls are symmetrical to one another. In each hall there is Royal Screen with Emperor's seat in red and gold color, there is a screen behind the seat with dragons roaming in clouds. Ordinary people are allowed to visit the halls. The corridors around the halls are used by people for betting by throwing coins on ground for food or money or other things and for showing. At the sides of the Immortal Bridge for pedestrians some people are trying to bet by throwing coins into a basin for money, clothes or other articles. People are bustling around the places.

At the south side of the bridge, there is a gate called Latticework Star Gate(Lin Xing Men). There are a pair of decorated stage buildings. When there is a competition held in the lake, prostitutes would stand on the stages. Across the gate at the south side of the street, there is a brick and stone dais, on the dais there are buildings which are about three hundred meters wide, it is called Treasure Ford Building(Bao Jin Lou). It is more than three hundred meters from the front of the dais to the gate of Gold Bright Lake. From the upper floor of the building, one could overlook Immortal Bridge and the five halls at the center of the lake. Emperor would sit at the upper floor of the building to watch horsemanship and archery and other activities.

At the east side of the lake, it is close to water, there are weeping willows around the wall. There are tents and screens at the sides of the road. At west side of the road, which are tents and screens close to lake, visitors could rent the tents or screens to watch competition in the lake; at the east side of the road, the tents and screens are used for food and liquor and other business activities and show business. Some tents are used as pawn shops. For pawned articles, if they are not redeemed before the lake is closed, the pawn shops will take the articles back to their shops to sell off.

You go north direction, you come to the back gate of the lake, it is West Water Gate of Bian River.

At the west bank of the lake, there are no buildings, only weeping willows are with verdant grasses along the bank, visitor rarely come to this side, but anglers like to come to area. The anglers must buy permits from the lake administration first. The visitors would buy the hooked fish with double price, the fishes would cut into thin slices, eat raw while drinking liquor, it is a delicious thing one rarely could bump into. When the navy finish their practising, they would moor the little dragon boats in the area.

At the north side of the lake, across the five halls at the center of the lake, there is a tall and wide building to store the big dragon boat, it is called 'Ao Wu'(Tall & Wide Building, it is believed the earliest shipyard in the world at that time).

Emperor usually arrives in Gold Bright Lake at March 20th. The soldiers of the security wears ornamental flowers on their heads, brocade uniform embroidered with golden thread with golden or silk waist bands. The uniforms of different companies compete for good looking appearances. They also take gold spears, jade adorned arrows and bows, banners embroidered with dragons and phoenixes, saddles and bridles with red tassels, thousands horses are galloping in the place, the ground is vibrating with the sounds of the bells and horse hooves.

Emperor Stays at Waterside Hall to Watch Competition and Hold Banquet for His Ministers

Emperor first comes to Waterside Hall to hold banquet for his ministers. There are tents erected in the lake at the front of the hall for Guard of Honor and Military Band. Near the hall in the lake there are four decorated boats lined in a column, soldiers are playing various games such as playing big banner, having lion dance, two fighting with broadsword with handles and shields and other comedies. Then there are another two boats for music bands, there is another boat with decorated small stage with three small doors just like the stage for puppet play across the boats of music bands.

The conductor comes forward to delivery greeting words. Music begins to play, the middle door in the front boat are opened, little puppets come out of the doors. In the boat there is a man with white clothes fishing in the lake, a young child is rowing the boat with a paddle, the little boat rows around for several times, the man with white clothes are delivering greeting words, music begins to play, the man gets a lively small fish from the lake. Music plays again, the small boat rows back to the colored tent. Then puppets come out to play kicking balls and tiptoe dancing etc., they deliver their greeting words, answer in concert with one another, play music etc, it is called Water Puppet(Shui Kui Lei). On the two decorated boats, there is a swing in the boat, at the bow an acrobat is climbing a pole, the royal musicians and instructors are beating drums and playing flutes to accompany the acrobat's show. Then another acrobat comes to play the swing, when the swing is about to come to level with the horizontal bar, the acrobat somersaults into water, it is called 'Water Swing'(Shui Qiu Qian). When the water play is over, the play boats and music bands boats begins to strike gongs and beat drums, people wave banners, leave the front of the building with the puppet boat from both sides.

There are twenty little dragon boats, there are fifty soldiers with red uniforms in each boat, there are command flag, drums and gongs in each boat. At the bow of the boat, there is a commander waving the flag for the navy. There are ten tiger boats, a man with brocade clothes is standing at the bow with a small flag, other people wear blue jackets. There are two fish boats painted in golden color, the boats look elegant. There are fifty people with colorful costumes waving colorful small flags and red umbrellas and striking small gongs and beating drums in each the boat. There are two small loach boats, the boat could hold only one man to row, they are dugouts contributed by Forward Zhu(Jin Zhu, an official responsible for finding and buying rare stones and transporting them to the capital from the south). All the small boats row to Ao Wu to pull the big dragon boat out of the building to the front of Waterside Hall. The little dragon boats are leading and rowing in front of the big dragon boats, the tiger boats are pulling the big dragon boat with ropes behind the little dragon boats.

The big dragon boat is about 100-120 meters long, 10-12 meters wide, the head and the tail of the boat are engraved fish scales and manes in golden color, the planks are painted with raw lacquer.. There are ten small rooms at the sides of the boat for his majesty's concubine to rest. There is an emperor's seat in the middle of the boat with dragon screen. The bottom plank is one hundred to one hundred twenty centimeters thick, there are iron coins as big as table spreading at the bottom of the boat to stabilize the boat from capsizing. There are several floors on the boat with halls and rooms and balustrades. There are seats for Emperor too in the halls. There is a commander waving flags at the bow of the boat, there are six oars stretching out of the boat from the side rowing room of the boat. When the oars are rowing, it seems the oars are flying over the water. The big boat is moored at one side of Waterside Hall when it arrives there.

Red flags are inserted into the lake in advance as marks from Waterside Hall to Immortal Bridge. The little dragon boats are standing in front and at the sides of Waterside Hall with bows facing each other. Tiger boats and fish boats are standing behind the dragon boats as if they are having a fight and are at flanks. In a short while, a commander standing at the top of the tent in front of Waterside Hall waves his red flags, the dragon boats would row out while beating drums and striking gongs, the boats would form a circle, it is called 'Round Battlefield Formation'(Xuan Luo); the commander waves his flag again, the boats would separate into two groups, each group forms its own round battlefield formation, it is called 'Sea Eyes'(Hai Yan); the commander waves his flag again, the boats would come forward and pass one another in opposite directions, it is called 'Crossing Bows'(Jiao Tou); the commander waves his flag again, the boats would line up at the east side of the five halls at the center of the lake facing Waterside Hall. Then a commander takes a long pole with colorful banners and a silver bowl hanging at its top end in a small boat, it is called 'Trophy'(Biao Gan), he would insert the pole into the water in front of Waterside Hall. The commander waves his flag again, then the sounds of drums and gongs come out of the dragon boats again, the boats rush forward to get the trophy. The fastest one gets the trophy, they would kneel down and kowtow to Emperor while shouting 'Long live Emperor', same competitions for tiger and fish boats. Then the small boats pull the big dragon boat back into Ao Wu again.

Emperor Visits Valuable Royal Garden

Emperor visits Valuable Royal Garden. The garden is located in the street of Obeying Heaven Gate facing northern direction across Gold Bright Lake. There are many old pine and cypress trees in weird forms along the street in front of the garden. There are pomegranate and cherry gardens at the sides of the garden with pavilions and stages, which are occupied by wine shops.

A hill of dozens meters high was built around the period of 1111-1115 AD, it is called Resplendent Orion Hill(Hua Zi Gang). There are magnificent halls, stages and pavilions boosting the wonderful images of one and another on the hill; there is a winding path paved by unique and expensive stones leading to the hill; there is a pond built of weird and invaluable stones from other places at the foot of the hill; there are weeping willow trees around the pond hiding the rainbow-like bridge over the pond; there are colorful flowers in rows and zones surrounding the big engraved and painted boat. The flowers include jasmine absolute, Arabian jasmine, morning star lily, winter daphne, banana shrub, thyme etc., the flowers from the south of the country like Fujian and Guangdong and Zhejiang. There are a moon pond, plum pavilion and peony pavilion etc. on the hill. There are so many pavilions on the hill, it is impossible to mention their names here.

Emperor's Trip to Treasure Ford Building

There is a rest palace at the south side of Treasure Ford Building. When Emperor visits Gold Bright Lake, the carriages for his Empress and concubines stop at the rest palace. No ordinary people are allowed to visit the place in ordinary time. At the west side of Treasure Ford Building, there is a hall to shoot arrow for Emperor, it is called Shooting Hall(She Dian). There is a street from east to west at the south of Treasure Ford Building, there are willow trees at the sides of the street. It is a place for people of the capital to play polo. You go to west, you come to the west gate of Valuable Royal Garden, a street at the south side of Navy Alley. There are old tung trees, small pavilions and stages at the sides of the street. You go to south, cross a small painted bridge, come to a pavilion with its pointed corners curving upward(Cuo Jiao Ting Zi), the pavilion is surrounded by a square pond which is enclosed by willow trees, it is called 'Frog Pavilion'(Ha Ma Ting), which is also taken as a wine shop.

At ordinary time when Emperor does not come to have a visit, the marines would practice on the ground in front of the gate of Valuable Royal Garden. When Emperor comes to have a visit, Royal Cavalry would stand at the sides of the gate. Along the walls at the sides of the gate, there are many platforms with colorful tents, ordinary people are allowed to stay in the tents to watch the show for Emperor by the soldiers. When Emperor goes to Gold Bright Lake, his personal guard would hold an yellow umbrella, his personal guards would whip along the way according to rites. Whenever the big dragon boat comes out or Emperor comes to the place, the number of visitors would double.

Emperor's Trip to Treasure Ford Building for Military Shows

When Emperor comes to Treasure Ford Building, the army would play in front of the building. First a dozen of drummers come out with their drums. A man with an instrument with two drum-shaped rattles in one piece comes out to deliver greeting words beginning with 'At the beginning of March' (Qing Chun San Yue, a melody from *For Small Stream in Hills*(Mu San Xi)). As soon as he finishes his singing, soldiers begin to beat drums and play flutes, a man with a red scarf begins to play with a big flag. Then lions and tigers enter the playground, they would jump, come forward, go backward, stand up and sit down in quick fashion. Then another man with a red scarf comes forward with two white flags, he whirls around like wind, it is called 'Puff Flag'(Pu Qi Zi). There are also shows for climbing pole and somersaulting etc. Then the band begins to play *Musician's Melody* (Qin Jia Long Ling). About a hundred soldiers with a makeup of peach or plum flower-like on their faces come forward with banners, pheasant feathers, wooden broad swords, shields. First they file rows to bow to Emperor, then switch their formations such as taking a bridge etc., in the end they form a crescent-like formation. The band begins to play *Shield's Melody*(Man Pai Ling), two soldiers come out of the crescent-like formation, they fight with each other, one rushes forward, one falls down backward to ground. Then five to seven pairs come out of the formation, they begin to fight with broad sword or sword against shield. Suddenly there is a loud cracking sound like thunder, it is called 'Firecracker'(Bao Zhang), then the soldiers retreat.

Fire and smoke break out, soldiers with mask and wigs come out, they are spewing out of smokes from their mouths as if they were ghosts or fairies. The soldiers wear blue tunic with golden flowers on the clothes and black trousers patched with golden pieces. They come out on bare feet, take big bronze gongs, dance forward and backward with music, it is called 'Hug Gongs'(Bao Luo). They would dance around the ground for several times, then set off fireworks etc. Another loud firecracker is setting off, the band begins to play *Bowing to Crescent Slowly*, soldiers painted with blue color on their faces come out with masks with golden eyes and leopard skin-like silk bands, they are called 'Ferocious Ghosts'(Ying Gui). They take broadswords, axes or wooden rods, step on tiptoes, and assume to seize, expel, observe or listen. Another loud bang of firecracker, there is a soldier with a mask and long beards, a green narrow gown, boots and clappers dressed like Kui Zhong (a famous immortal of Taoist who is good at catching ghosts), there is a man with a little gong accompanying him to dance, he is called 'Dance Companion'(Wu Pan). Then two to three extremely thin men come out, their faces were painted white with golden eyes as if they were skeletons. They wear broad colorful waist bands, take soft sticks, falter around in ridiculous fashion as if they were playing farce, it is called 'Pantomime'(Ya Za JU). Then another loud bang of firecracker, fire and smoke rush out, you could not see the faces of the performers even if you stand close to them. There are seven performers standing in the smoke. They have loose hairs with tattoo-like figures on their blue gauze tunic and broad colorful waist bands. One of them wears a small cap with golden flowers with a white banner in his hand, others wear scarves, take real broadswords in their hands, fight with one another as if they wanted to cut other's face and take out other's heart, they are called 'Seven Mighty Broadswords'(Qi Shen Dao). Another loud bang of firecracker, fire and smoke break out. When smoke dies down, one could see blue screen around the place, dozens of soldiers are standing around with face masks and bizarre clothes, as if they were statutes of immortals and ghosts seen in a temple, it is called 'Finishing Screen'(Xie Zhang). Another loud bang of firecracker, the screens are rolled up, the performers retreat.

Next a man is striking a little bronze gong and leads about a hundred soldiers coming out to show. They wear scarves or are with double buns for their hairs, wear motley clothes of short sleeves and broad waistbands. Their faces are powdered yellow or white, it is called 'Staggering Smear'(Mo Qiang). They each take a broadsword with a long handle, and form lines. The man with the gong shouts order to them, they pay their greeting to Emperor. Then with orders they change their formations from this to that, they fight with each other with hitting or piercing. In the end one man of the pair throws down his broadsword, plumps down onto the ground heavily on back, it is called 'Falling Plank'(Ban Luo). Then other performers follow the suit. Then a man with peasant clothes comes to the ground, he first delivers his greeting words, then a woman with peasant clothes comes to the ground, she bumps into with the man, they fight each other with sticks as if they were having a real fight. Then the man carries the woman out on his stick. Then the band begins to play, the soldiers from various units come together to play a piece of comedy. Then folk performers come together to play another a piece of comedy. Famous artists such as Stay Xiao(ZhuEr Xiao), CapitalContest Ding(DuSai Ding), ElderDaughter Xue(ZiDa Xue), YoungerDaughter Xue(ZiXiao Xue), Cherish Yang(ZongXi Wang), ForLongevity Cui(ShangShou Cui) etc. would take part in the show.

After the show, the internal guards of Royal Palace begin to have horse show. First a man rides on a horse with empty hands, it is called 'Leading Horse'(Yin MA). Then another man rides on a horse while waving a flag, it is called 'Clearing Flag'(Kai Dao Qi). Then another man rides on a horse with a red embroidered ball and a long red rope, the ball is pulling along the ground. Several men on horses are chasing after the ball with bows, the men shooting with left hand are called 'Yang Shou She'(Yang She Shou), the men with right hand 'He Shou She'(He She Shou). Then willow branches are inserted in the ground, several men on horses shoot the branches with different bows, it is called 'Chop Willow'(Zha Liu). Then a man carrying a windmill inserted with a dozen little flags comes out a horse, it is called

'Hurricane Flags'(Xuan Feng Qi). Then a man comes out while standing on a horse, it is called 'Standing Horse'(Li Ma). Or a man jumps down from a horse, then jumps back on the horse again, it is called 'Side Horse'(Pian Ma). Or a man catches the stirrup in his hand, moves his body back on the horse, it is called 'Jump Horse'(Tiao Ma). Or a man suddenly let his body leave the saddle, uses his right foot to hang himself up on the place of the neck of the horse, his left foot insert into the stirrup, his left hand catch the mane, it is called 'Dedicate Saddle'(Xian An) or 'Sit Backward'(Qi Zong Bei Zuo). Or a man catch the stirrups in his hands, use his shoulders to stand on saddles, stretch his legs into air, it is called 'Stand Upside Down'(Dao Li). Or a man puts his foot on ground, is pulled along the ground, then jumps on the back of the horse again, it is called 'Catch Horse'(Gan Ma). Or a man steps the stirrup with his left foot, takes his right foot out, his body stays at the side of the horse, his right hand catches the saddle and his left hand catches the mane to stabilize his body, stretch his right leg while running on a horse, it is called 'Flying Immortal Catching a Horse'(Fei Xian Fu Ma); or hiding his body at one side of the horse, it is called 'Hiding in Stirrup'(Deng Li Cang Shen); or catching the saddle with both hands while pulling his feet on the ground, it is called 'Drive Horse'(Gan Ma); or one foot leaves the stirrup, one drops his body down, catches the strap, touches the ground with his hand, it is called 'Grab Dust'(Chuo Chen); or letting the horse run in front of him, he chases the horse, catches the horsetail first, then jumps on the horse back, it is called 'Leopard Horse'(Bao Zi Ma); or lying horizontally on horse back while waving sword, broadsword, or sword with double edges etc. Then the horse show comes to an end.

Then several old soldiers with yellow clothes leads in front with little flags embroidered with dragons, they are followed by several hundred palace maids on horses, they are called 'Beautiful Girls Team'(Miao Fa Yuan Nv Tong). They dress up like men, with short scarf, tunic made from imported colorful satin embroidered by golden threads, with green or red waist bands. The horses are with jade halters, golden bits, expensive saddles and luxurious saddle pads, the palace maids and their horses are glittering under bright sun, fragrant wind is blowing to nostrils of people from them. The team gallops to the front of Waterside Hall, run around for several times, with elegant and light beating of drums, some of them begin to play horse show. Eunuch Hunt Li(Tian Li) as a commander leads the girls into lines, upon hearing the drum beat, they all jump down from the horses, with one hand holding bow and another holding rein, they salute Emperor by kneeling down to ground like men while shouting 'Long Live Emperor'. After the salutation, they jump back on horse back again upon hearing drum beat. As the maids dress up like men, thus they salute like men. Then they gallop back and forth, gather up and disperse out to change their formations. Then they form two groups, they fight in pairs on horse backs by shooting arrows or with sticks or spears as if they were fighting in real battlefield. After the valiant show, the girls retreat with their horses.

The band begins to play music again. A festooned polo gate is set up in front of Waterside Hall, about one hundred men wear scarves with their ends of the scarf bending backward, half of them wear red coat and the other wear blue coat, the coats are with horizontal bands, tie their waists with bands, wear silk shoes, ride on donkeys with colorful saddles and beautiful saddle pads. They form two teams, each team has a leader, they take festooned polo clubs, it is called 'Little Hit'(Xiao Da, as the competition takes place with donkeys). One commander hits the ball, it seems that the ball is stuck on the club. As soon as the ball falls down onto ground from the club, the teams begin to chase after the ball and pass the ball to their commander. The left team tries to hit the ball into the gate, the right team tries to prevent the ball to get into the gate. They chase one after another, in the end the one with highest chips win the game, Emperor would give the team a reward. Then several soldiers with yellow clothes lead more than one hundred eunuchs coming out to play the ball. They follow the same rule as before, but they ride on little horses with jade jewelry ornaments, jade belt and red boots, it is called 'Big Hit'(Da Da). They all are good at riding, gallop on the horses like fairies elegantly and beautifully, one could only see such a kind of scene in paintings. Then the military show comes to an end.

Emperor's Trip To Shooting Hall

Emperor goes to Shooting Hall. There are two dozens of soldiers of Arrow Shooting Company of Royal Guard standing in front of the target. They wear scarves with long ends with violet embroidered headbands, violet loose coats with yellow horizontal bands. They line up like flying wild geese. When Emperor shoots an arrow, the soldiers would shout hurrah while dancing, they gather together, then disperse again. At the moment, the arrow has already hit its target. Then a soldier hold a silver bowl in his mouth, takes one bowl each in his hands, sets one bowl each on his shoulders, thus there are total five silver bowls. When arrows come forward, he would take the arrow into his bowls. After the shooting, Emperor returns to Waterside Hall.

Games in Valuable Royal Garden

Besides liquor shops and show people, various tents are taken up by businessmen who are doing betting games. Various jades, antiques, rare articles, silk cloth, daily articles, tea and liquor utensils are spreading on the ground as bets. Sometimes the odd ratio is about one to thirty, thus people could bet on horse, carriage, land and house, housemaids, dancing girls with a price set beforehand. They provide gambling paraphernalia for people, BigHead Ren(DaTou Ren), Joyful Third(Kui Huo San) are the most famous gamblers, others are too many to mention their names.

The administration of Gold Bright Lake and Valuable Royal Garden offers fish, lotus root and other produces to Emperor, Emperor gives them to his ministers accordingly. Royal Workshops offer little dragons, etched elephant tusk, engraved jade and other ornamental things to Emperor, they really are beautiful and elegant.

Performers who follow Emperor to play in the scene are ManySkills Zhang(YiDuo Zhang), ManyEyes(Hun Shen Yan), ForeverFragrance Song(ShouXiang Song) and CalmScholar Yin(ShiAn, Yin) for small music instruments, OuterCalm Li for water puppet, others are too many to mention here from period 1111-1125 AD.

The foods sold in Gold Bright Lake include: Rice in soup, green pea soup, snail meat with free plum wine, hawthorn slice, apricot slice, preserved plum, fragrant crispy plum, sashimi on spot, black carp, salty duck egg, pickles etc.

At the end of the show in Gold Bright Lake, the rich would take their own boats back into their homes, wrap the boats with violet screen, put into the pond for their singers and dancers. In the period between 1111 and 1125 AD, ordinary people are allowed to rent boats in the lake for fun, the rent depends on the size and kind of a boat.

Emperor's Return to Royal Palace

Emperor would ride a horse when he returns to Royal Palace from Gold Bright Lake. Emperor would wear a hat with flowers inserted on his cap. All the ministers, officials, personal guards and guards of honor are rewarded with flowers. In one year, Emperor took a white horse and came to the front of Supreme Harmony Taoist Temple, suddenly called his little black horse. The horse came to the front of Emperor, but it did not go further. His attendant said:"He hopes to be awarded with a title." Then Emperor gave it a title of General Galloping Dragon(Long Xiang Jiang Jun), then the horse followed obediently with a lead. Emperor awarded the title to the horse because he loved the horse very much.

In those days the capital was filled with colorful things, everywhere was shiny, royal scent could be smelled everywhere, everywhere was filled with joyful and happy music, treasured horses were galloping in streets, streets were filled with festooned tents. Every household was adorned with jade and silk, as if immortals were living there; every home was a painted palace, as if they were fairies' palace. Whether scholars or ordinary people, they all took carriages or rode on horses, the carriages and horses were hundred thousands. Prostitutes usually took donkeys, but in the period between 1111-1125 AD, they all rode on horses, they wore thin clothes and veils, they would tie the veils on their hairs. Young whore visitors followed them on horses with thin clothes and caps. Several young dandies with tattoos manipulated their horses, the horses were called 'Flowers Horses'(Hua Tui Ma). They would force the horses to walk with their heads nearly touching the ground with short rein, it was called 'Rein Martingale'(Yang Jiang). Those daddies shouted loudly, galloped their horses on streets to compete for speed. Visitors would shoulder the things they won in the games to return to their homes. The ladies of rich families took palanquins, the palanquins were adorned with flowers, the screens of the palanquins were drawn up. From March 1ˢᵗ to April 8ᵗʰ, even in rainy or windy day, visitors still came to Gold Bright Lake.

The month is late in spring, flowers are booming everywhere, peony, common peony, kerria, banksia rose and other flowers are sold in markets. The sellers would put flowers into bamboo basket shaped like a horse head, chanted in an elegant and charming way for selling flowers. If one stays in a quiet courtyard, warm sunlight shines onto curtains, or at the top floor of the house, morning glow shines on bed drape, the person is still waking up from the hangover, when he hears the calling sound, it could easily touch the sensitive heart strings, create new sorrow and sadness. The moment is the most wonderful time in one's life. In the month the army stationed in the capital will leave the city and go to suburbs to have drills for battle formations and other training.

Volume Eight

April Eighth

April 8th, it is birthday of Buddha, the biggest ten Buddhist temples will hold the ceremony to bath Buddha statute with scented water. The temples would boil scented sugar water, give to people coming to the ceremony, the scented water is called 'Buddha Bathing Water'.

Gradually day becomes longer, the weather becomes mild and clear. In the courtyard with blooming pomegranate flowers, one could hear the courting sound of yellow warblers from time to time; in the pavilion surrounded by waving willow trees, occasionally could see swallows taking their fledglings flying around. The seventy two famous restaurants in the capital begin to sell newly brewed wines, everyone gets excited by the sale. Particularly Cool Breeze Restaurant at the south of the capital is the best place to have a drink in summer. People could taste green apricot and have cherry. When friends meet, people begin to drink happily.

In the month, people begin to sell eggplant and squash. The first place to sell eggplant and squash is in the market at East Magnificent Gate, a pair could be sold for thirty to fifty thousands coins. Seasonable fruits include plum, golden apricot, royal peach etc.

May Fifth

In May 5th festival one could buy: Five colors knitted thread ornaments, wormwood flowers for hair-dress from real wormwood leaves or paper, shaking rattle, flowers painted fan, sugar preserved fruits, glutinous rice and other stuffs wrapped with bamboo leaves(Zong Zi), steamed wheat flour round bun; basil, sweet flag, and cockle papaya could be chopped finely, mixed with scents, placed in plum red boxes.

From May 1st to 4th, people begin to sell peach, willow branch, hollyhock flower, sweet flag leaves and folium artemisiae argyi. At May 5th, the things would be put at the entrance of every household with glutinous rice and other stuffs wrapped with bamboo leaves, rice dumpling, tea and wine as articles of tribute. People would nail a scarecrow made of folium artemisiae argyi at the door. Scholars and ordinary people would hold banquets for their friends.

June 6th Birthday of Immortal Cui and June 24th Birthday of Immortal Erlang

June 6th, Birthday of Immortal Cui in Taoist temple at the north side of the capital. People dedicate a lot of articles of tribute to the Immortal, it has never been so prosperous in the temple.

June 24th, Birthday of Immortal Erlang at the west side of the capital (Erlang Sheng is a powerful god in controlling flood and fighting against ghost and devils to Taoist), a lot of people go to celebrate his birthday. The temple of Erlang Sheng is outside of Victories Gate, it is called Blessing God Taoist Temple by an imperial decree.

In June 23rd, Royal Palace send articles of tribute to the temple, the articles include polo club, slingshot, instruments to shoot fowls and beasts, saddles, bridles, cages etc. from Royal Palace Workshops and Book Bureau, all are elegant and beautiful things. Military Band is playing and leading the procession to the temple. A temporary stage is set up in front of the temple, Royal Bands and Military Band are playing music on the stage, other comedies and dancing are taking turns. Worship Officials Bureau of Royal Palace provide twenty four dishes for tribute according to certain sequences all the day and night on.

In June 24th, people rush forward at three o'clock in the morning to burn the first incenses in the temple according to custom. Some people would sleep in the temple, thus they could burn first incenses to the statute. At daybreak, various bureaus and people in various professions come to pay tribute. A lot of shows take place on the stage, tens thousands articles and things are dedicated to the statue. From the early morning, people start to play various shows on the stage such as climbing pole, jumping, wire-walking, wrestling, clapper and drum beating, cock fighting, funny talking, short play to make people laugh, riddle guessing, storytelling, acrobats, playing with dummy, sounds imitating, peddlers' calling imitating, ghost playing with face mask, puppet playing, magic show etc. The shows last in the evening. There are two banner poles of dozens meters high erected in front of the temple. The left pole is provided by Capital Workshop(Jing Cheng Suo), and the right pole by Maintenance Department. Artists would climb on the poles to show their skills, someone would place a wood on the top of the pole, stand on the wood to play ghosts while spewing out smoke and fire. It is very dangerous and frightening. The shows end at nightfall.

Various Things Sold In June

In June one could buy: at the entrances of alleys and markets, one could buy cooked rice in soup, roasted meat, dried meat, asparagus lettuce, pickled leaf mustard, sweet melon from Yi Tang(Right Pond) Village, golden peach from Nanjing, crispy pear, golden apricot, plum from Xu Prefecture, tender water chestnut, papaya, ice cold lychee paste. All the things are put on a bed supported by benches and under the shade of a blue cloth umbrella.

For ice cold things, the best ones are two stands out of Old Song Gate, they provide the things with silverware: sweet pea soup, sugared Chinese honey locust seed, stuffed round millet ball, gorgon fruit, chicken skin with sesame-starch mixture looking like bean curd, jellied sesame-starch mixture looking like jellied bean curd, skewered fruit on bamboo stick, sesame ball, fried wheat flour ball stuffed with cowpea paste, fried wheat flour ball stuffed with red bean paste etc.

People of the capital pay high attention to the three ten-day hottest period as there is no other festival in June. Usually pavilions at waterside and high buildings are best places for people to visit. People would put melons and plum and other fruits into cold water with ice, drink at the stream with flowing cups down the water, eat preserved fish in fresh lotus leaves, no matter where, one could hear beautiful sound of singing and music, the activity could last all night.

July 7th

July 7th is the festival for seventh night in seventh month(a legendary love story between a cowboy and one of the daughters of the Queen of Heaven).

Businessmen sell clay statutes of Mahoraga (praying for giving birth a boy) in East Street of Pan's Restaurant, Entertainment Area of outside Liang Gate at the west side of the capital, outside of North Gate, the street outside of Rosefinch Gate, Horse Walk Street. The statute is set on a stand made of engraved and painted wood, or put into a red gauze lantern, or adorned with gold, jade, pearl or elephant tusk, a pair of statues cost about several thousands coins for expensive ones. The officials working in Royal Palace, the rich and the ordinary all take the statute as an essential for the day. People would cast wild goose, mandarin duck, violet mandarin duck, turtle, fish etc. with beeswax, then painted with various colors, it is called 'Float on Water'(Shui Shang Fu). People would put soil on a wood plank, plant millet seed, let the seedlings grow, then put cottages, flowers and trees, and figurines of farmers on the plank, it is called 'Grain Plank'(Gu Ban). People would carve melon into various things, it is called 'Melon Flower'(Hua Gua). People would use oil, flour, sugar and honey as ingredients to make little smiling cake, it is called 'Deserts'(Guo Shi), the cake could be made in stick-like or two squares overlapped pattern. If one wants to buy 500 g of the deserts, the seller would include a pair of figurine made of the same material with armors which look like door-god. The custom is moved on but none knows when and why it was started, the pair of figurine are called 'Deserts General'(Guo Shi Jiang Jun). People would put green pea, red bean and wheat into a ceramic container in water to let them germinate, when they grow to a dozen centimeters, the seedlings would be tied with red and blue threads, it is called 'Plant

Birth'(Zhong Sheng). All these are seasonable things for the festival, and sold in festooned tents in streets.

Three to five days before the holiday, streets are filled with horses, carriages and people with silk clothes. People would pick lotus flowers, make a pair with the flowers to have fun. They would take the flowers back to their home, when other people see the flowers, they would marvel for the beauty. Children would buy new lotus leaves and imitate the style of the clay statutes of Mahoraga. Children would wear new colorful and beautiful clothes for the imitation and compete for their appearances.

In nights of July 6th and 7th, the rich would put up a decorated archway in their courtyards, it is called 'Pray Adroitness Building'(Qi Qiao Lou). They would dedicate the clay statutes of Mahoraga, carved melon, wine and meat, writing brush and paper, needlework, or poems written by their children, or things made by girls, they would burn incenses and bow to the statute, it is called 'Pray Adroitness'(Qi Qiao). In the night, women would put thread through the eye of a needle, or would put a spider into a box. In next morning they would open the box, if the spider spins a neat web, then it means they get the adroitness, it is called 'Get Adroitness'(De Qiao). Households and brothels would put various articles at their entrances to compete for luxury.

July Fifteenth

July fifteenth is Zhong Yuan Jie(Mid Origin Festival, it is also called ghost day. It is said in the day the king of the hell will pardon some ghosts and let the ghosts have a rebirth as human again for next life).

Several days before the festival, businessmen begin to sell paper things for the dead: shoes, boots, scarf, hat, golden and rhinoceros horn waist band, and clothes in various colors, Peddlers sell the things along streets. Pan's Restaurant Street, East Area of the capital, West Entertainment Area, just like July Seventh, businessmen would sell deserts, Plant Birth and various flowers and fruits too. People also sell printed Usnisa Vijaya Dharani Sutra(A sutra about of pardoning a king after he died) and the script of Maudgalyayana about hungry ghost(a sutra about the causes of being a hungry ghost). People would use cut bamboos to make a three feet stand about 100 centimeters in height, the top is weaved into a form like a bowl, it is called Yu Lan Peng(Hang Upside Down Bowl, it is said when people die, they would suffer by being hung upside down for their sins committed in their lives), people would put paper clothes and money on top to burn for their dead relatives to save them from the suffering. The artists in Entertainment Area begin to play 'Save Mother by Maudgalyayana' till Fifteenth. A lot of people go to watch the play. One day before the Fifteenth, people begin to sell the leaves of chinaberry tree, the leaves are used to spread on the table when people pay tributes to their ancestors. People would tie nests made of hemp and straw at the feet of the table, that means to pray to their ancestors for blessing their harvests in fall. People also sell cockscomb flower, the flower is also dedicated to their ancestors on the table, it is called 'Wash Hand Flower'(Xi Shou Hua) as people have to wash their hands when they put the flower on the table for their ancestors.

In Fifteenth, vegetarian foods are dedicated to ancestors. At daybreak, peddlers begin to sell prosomillet rice from door to door, people use the rice to dedicate to their ancestors to mean they would have a good harvest, peddlers also sell cauliflower, fried pancake, stuffed pancake etc. If one family has a newly buried grave, they would go to sweep the grave in the day outside of the city. Royal Palace would send people in carriage to pay tributes to the tombs in various temples. Temples would hold large praying ceremonies with the permits of the government to pray for died soldiers to let them have rebirth to human from ghosts with burning mountains-like paper money.

Beginning of Autumn

In the day of Beginning of Autumn, people begin to sell leaves of Chinese catalpa, women and children would cut the leaves into various forms and put them on their hairs.

In the month, a lot of melons, fruits, pears and jujube begin to sell in market. There are several kinds of jujube in the capital: Big sweet one, pointed one like a tooth, one from Qin Prefecture and one from Bo Prefecture. Gorgon fruit is on market too. The best one is Harmony Li's (He Li) within Liang Gate. The powerful, the eunuchs and the royal family would buy from the shop. The shop would put them in a golden box, and give it to the eunuch to deliver to Royal Palace everyday. For scholars and ordinary people, a pack is about ten coins, the gorgon fruit is wrapped with fresh lotus leaves sprinkled with musk and tied with red thread. Many shops sell the fruit, only Harmony Li's is the best as they only sell selected silver tender ones.

Sacrifice to God of Land

In August, there is a sacrifice ceremony to God of Land(Qiu She, about forty days after the day of Beginning of Autumn), people would use Sacrifice Cake and Liquor as gifts. The relatives of Emperor, the concubines of Emperor would use pork, mutton, kidney, breast, intestine, lung, duck and ginger as ingredients, cook the ingredients into a chess-like form, after basting with appropriate seasonings, the pieces would put on the top of rice, it is called Sacrifice Rice (She Fan), and the rice is used to host guests and for sacrifice.

Married woman would return to her parents' home. When she comes back in evening, grandparents, aunts and uncles would give gourds and jujubes newly marketed as gift to her son, it is called 'Benefit Nephew' (Yi Liang Wai Shen) as people believe the things would bring luck to her son.

Teachers of private school begin to collect tuition from their students to use the money to host various parties through hiring help hands and singers. When teachers come back from the parties, they would take flower basket, fruits, foods and sacrifice cake. The activity repeats in Spring Sacrifice, May Fifth and Nine Ninth.

Mid-Autumn Festival

Before Mid-Autumn Festival, all restaurants begin to sell newly brewed wines, reconstruct the decorated archways, redecorate their flag poles and hang new flags with drunk immortals. People would come to restaurants to drink, around one or two o'clock in afternoon, all wines in the restaurants are sold out, the restaurants have to draw down their flags to signal no wine is left. At the time, crab is on market, so do pomegranate, hard pear, pear, chestnut, grape, orange etc.

In the night, the rich and powerful would sit in newly decorated pavilions, ordinary people would rush to restaurants to occupy best spots to watch moon. For households near Royal Palace, people could hear music sound coming out of the palace late in night, as if the sound were from paradise. Children would play in alleys for all night, night markets are bustling with people and last for whole night.

Nine Ninth

September 9th is Nine Ninth Festival

People appreciate chrysanthemums in the day. There are several kinds of chrysanthemums: those with yellowish white flower petals and pistil looking like lotus seedpod are called 'Longevity Chrysanthemums'(Wan Ling Ju); those with pink petals are called 'Peach Chrysanthemums'(Tao Hua Ju); those with white petals and pink pistils are called 'Banksia Rose Chrysanthemums'(Mu Xiang Ju); those with yellow petals and round flowers are called 'Gold Bell Chrysanthemums'(Jin Ling Ju); those with white petals and big flowers are called 'Beautiful Looking Chrysanthemums'(Zhen Rong Ju).

People would go to high places in suburbs for party. The places include King Cang's Temple (A legendary inventor of Chinese characters), Two Kilometers Bridge, Sorrow Dais(Chou Tai), Hui Wang Liang's Old City (Liang Wang Chen, a king of Wei State in 400-319 BC), Inkstone Dais(A burial ground for Yi Zhang who was a strategist and politician in Warring Period?~ 309BC), Camel Hill(A place for raising horses for Royal Palace) and Lone Happiness Hill (A burial ground for the famous prime minister Dan Wang of Song Dynasty 957-1017 AD).

One or two days before the festival, people would send gift of flour cakes to one another, little colorful flags would be inserted onto the cake with pomegranate seeds, chestnuts, ginkgo seeds, pine seeds etc. People also put figurines of lion and barbarian king made of flour on the top too.

Temples hold praying ceremonies. Only Open Treasure Buddhist Temple and Kind King Buddhist Temple(Ren Wang Si) hold lion pray ceremonies. Monks would sit on lion bed (a place sitting by senior monks is called lion bed) to pray and talk about scriptures, the temples have the largest numbers of visitors.

In the latter part of the month, people begin to buy paper clothes, boots, shoes and cloth to be burnt to their ancestors in October 1st.

Volume Nine

October 1st

In October 1st, Emperor rewards winter clothes to officials lower than Prime Minister. October 5th, scholars and ordinary people of the capital go out of the city to pay tributes to their ancestors' graves. Royal Palace would send people in carriages to various temples to pay tributes, also send people to go to Royal Temples at West Capital(Current Luoyang). The carriages and horses of the relatives of Emperor also go to various temples to pay tribute just like in Cold Food Day. Governments would deliver charcoals to Royal Palace for winter. Ordinary people would hold party to start their heating stoves.

Peaceful Heaven Festival

October 10th, Peaceful Heaven Festival, it is birthday of Emperor Hui Zong(Excellent Ancestor). One month before the day, Royal Band will call royal musicians together to prepare for the occasion. October 8th, the minister of defense will take all officers above regiment commander; October 10th, the primer minister of state council will take all officials above seventh grade in rank to go to Assist State Buddhist Temple to take part in a vegetarian party holding in the temple to celebrate the birthday. At the end of party, the officials would go to the auditorium of State Council to take part in a banquet held on the behalf of Emperor.

Congratulating Birthday by Prime Minister, Princes and Officials in Royal Palace

October 12th, Prime Minister, Princes, Relatives of Emperor, Officials go into Royal Palace to congratulate the birthday, all people kowtow for seven times (in ordinary times only for two times). All of them hold their tablets(As an official symbol, people could jot something down on it, otherwise it could be inserted around waist band), follow the rites to see Emperor.

Before music plays, artists of Royal Band begin to imitate birds' chirping on the festooned stage in front of Gather Outstanding People Hall. Except the chirping, everywhere is quiet. People could hear the chirping sound of the birds coming from sky, as if phoenixes were chirping gladly in the palace. Officials take their seats after greeting, Prime Minister, senior ministers, princes, relatives of Emperor and Commanders of Army , envoys and deputy envoys of Great Khitan State, Korea and Xia State have seats within Gather Outstanding People Hall. Heads of various departments and bureaus and attending people of the envoys have seats at the corridors of the hall. Commanders below division level will have seats at the back of the festooned building.

For the party, short black lacquered tables with red tops are used with short stool with blue cushion. On each table there are ring pancakes like a bracelet, deep-fried pancake, jujube cake like a tower etc. as decorating deserts, various fruits are put on the table too. Only the table taken by the envoys of Great Khitan State has meats of pork, mutton, chicken, goose, rabbit etc. with bones. All the meats are tied with thin thread. The meats are served with small plates of green onions, chives, garlic and vinegar. Three to five people share one pail of soup with several ladles. Two leaders of Royal Band stand at the side of the festooned stage(wearing scarves in funny fashion, loose violet gown, golden waist and colored gown band) are in charge of pouring wines in the banquet. When attendant is pouring wine to Emperor, they would raise both of their long sleeves, shout 'pour wine to Emperor', as soon as they finish their callings, they would touch the railings lightly with their sleeves. When attendants are pouring wine to ministers, they would short 'pour wine', they raise and put down their sleeves like before.

Royal Band stay in the tent under the stage. All musicians wear scarves with long ends, wear their corresponding uniforms in violet, red or green with wide sleeves and golden concave belts. In front column are ten clappers, next lines are fifty pipa players with painted pipa (a four strings plucked instrument), two harps are in next line. The harp is about one point two meters high, looks like half of a comb, is painted black with engraved flowers in golden color, is setting on a stand. There are twenty five strings per harp, one player kneels down and plays with his both hands in a hugging fashion. Next line are two big drums on colored base with golden dragons. The drum beater ties his loose sleeves on his back, wears tight yellow sleeves with hanging silk bands on his hands, his drum sticks are wrapped with gold, he raises his drum sticks high to beat the drum as if a shooting star were flying by. Next line are two Jie Drum(A drum could be beaten at two sides wrapped with ram skin and a slender waist), looks like ordinary drums used by foreign people, and are put on little tables. The drum is beaten with two sticks). Next are chime irons which are hung on a bright colored stand with tassels. The next are vertical bamboo flutes, reed pipe wind instruments, egg-shaped holed wind instruments, flutes, bamboo oboes with nine holes, and dragon flutes. There are two hundred Zhang Drums(Zhang drum is beating at the right side with a stick and the left side with a hand), the player of Zhang drums wear scarves with long ends, violet silk head bands, violet loose gown with back knot, yellow tight sleeves, tassels and yellow bands. Play performers wear scarves in funny fashion, corresponding violet, red or green loose gowns, golden waist bands. They stand in pairs facing each other from the front of the steps of the hall to the front of the festooned stage. When players enter the stage, these two lines of people would cross their hands in front of their chests, shrug their shoulders, step on their feet, dance together with the music, they are called 'Massage Tune'(Ruo Qu Zi).

First cup: when an attendant is pouring wine to Emperor, a singer sings first song for '*Zhong Qiang*' (baritone) once, then accompany by vertical bamboo flutes, reed pipe wind instruments and flutes; then chorus, then the singer sings solo again. When an attendant is pouring wine to Prime Minister, music band plays '*pour cups*'; for officials, music band plays '*Three Dais Tune*'(San Tai Ling).The solo dancer is MidCelebration Lei(ZhongQing Lei), other accompanying dancers wear scarves in funny fashion with loose clothes, as MidCelebration Lei is with an official title, thus he dances in his official uniform. When the music plays to Po, Dian tunes(Two tunes out of eight tunes for an official ceremony), solo dancers comes out to dance; when the music comes to an ending, another dancer joins in, they play together for several pats, then the first dancer retreats, the later dancer dance till the end of the music, he is called 'End Dancer'(Wo Mo).

Second cup: For Emperor's wine, singing likes before; for Prime Minister's wine, the tune is called *Slow Tune*(Man Qu Zi); for officials, the tune is still '*Three Dais Tune*'.

Third cup: Left and right armies come out to play on stage. The so-called left and right armies are not the soldiers of Royal Guard. They are folk artists coming from the left and the right areas of the capital. The play include climbing pole, wire-walking, standing upside down, playing dices in bowl, spinning bowls on a rod, walking heads on by two performers, somersaulting etc. without using live lions and leopards, playing big flag and ghosts. The performers include men and women, they all wear red clothes and bright clothes. There are big holes in the huge stones in front of the hall, thus as soon as people come out, they would set up poles for the play. When Emperor holds a banquet, only from third cup, there are dishes for drinking with wines: fried pork with fermented soybean paste, fried meat and roasted dumpling looks like humps of a camel.

Fourth cup: The music repeats like before. At the end of the dance, the performers would make a farce, The announcer of Royal Band would hold a bamboo stick and a horsetail whisk in his hands, deliver his greeting words and psalm, other players accompany him; then he delivers another greeting words with other things. Foods for wine drinking: Roasted mutton ribs with skin and bone, bean jelly, pressed pork without fat, sesame pancake.

Fifth cup: for Emperor, solo Pipa; for primer minister, solo chime irons. For solo players, the players come to the hall, after pay their tributes to Emperor, they would play in the hall. For officials, Royal Band plays '*Three Dais Tune*' as before. At the end of the music, The announcer of Royal Band holds a bamboo stick, delivers greeting words for Children Dancers. The ages for children are about 12 to 13 years old, about 200 hundred children forming four rows. Each row has a leader accompanied by four children. All children wear little hermit caps with red, green, violet and blue bright uniforms, the collar has four slits, they wear scarves with rolled corners with banners on their uniforms and waist bands, take flowers in their hands and stand in rows. First four children carry a banner with the name of their team in golden characters in violet uniforms and scarves, come forward under drum beating. There is a couplet on the banner: *Waving phoenixes under Jiu Shao*(a music made by Shun, a very ancient emperor in legendary), *Waving blue birds under Ba Yi* (a music used for Emperor in Zhou Dynasty 1046-256 BC). Royal Band play music, the dancers come forward to front of the steps of the hall, kowtow to Emperor. The announcer of Royal Band delivers greeting words for Children

Dancers, the leaders of the dancers come forward to shout greeting slogans, other players accompany them in greeting at the sides. After the greeting, Royal Band begins to play music again. The dancers chant with the music while dancing, then begin to sing '*Po Zi*'(An episode of a music under such an occasion). At the end of the singing, the leaders of dancers come forward to recite greeting words and librettos of plays and lead the dancers onto stage, the play has two segments. At the moment the famous actors of play of Royal Band include Distended Turtle(Bi Peng) , Qiao Liu(Play Liu), PrimaryPlayer Hou(BoChao Hou), FirstScene Meng(JinChu Meng), YanXi Wang(SmileFace Wang), they all are leaders and deputy leaders of the play of Royal Band. For the play within the hall, as envoys are present, the play could not do in an utterly funny way. Only several dancers come into the hall, they dance with acrobat styles in funny fashion. When play comes to an end, The announcer of Royal Band delivers '*Little Dancers*' greeting words, lead the little dancers on the stage, they dance under '*Ying Tian Chang*'(Greet Heaven Long) . Dishes for wine include: Roasted meats, Heaven Flower Cakes, Roasted Cakes stuffed with minced meat or vegetables, shredded meat soup, flower-like cakes. Emperor stands up to leave the seat to have a short break, officials come out of the hall and have a rest in tents out of the hall. In a short moment, the officials come back and greet Emperor according to their ranks, then take their seats.

Sixth cup: for Emperor's wine, reed pipe wind instruments play solo for slow pace tune; for Prime Minister's wine, same slow tune; for officials same '*Three Dais Tune*'. Soldiers of Left and Right Companies begin to erect ball gate in front of the hall. The gate is about ten meters high, festooned with colorful bands, netted around with only an opening about thirty centimeters in front. The leader of the left team is Talk Su(Shu Su) with a scarf of long ends, red brocade uniform, his ten team members all wear scarves with rolled ends and red brocade uniform; the leader of the right team is Communicate Meng(Xuan Meng), he and his ten members all wear blue brocade uniforms. Royal

Band begins with a whistling sound, then Zhang drums play the music for the teams. Left team first play the ball, pass the ball to their players, everyone would kick one or two times; two deputy leaders kick several more times, then pass the ball to the leader, the leader kicks the ball into the gate. Right team gets the ball, pass the ball to their players, everyone kicks one or two times, then pass the ball to two deputy leaders who kick the ball for several times, then pass the ball to the leader who kicks the ball into the gate like the leader of the left team. Emperor will award the winner with silver bowl and bolts of brocade, the players would kowtow to Emperor for his reward. All the players would cover their bodies with the brocade from Emperor when they kowtow to Emperor. The leader of the lost team would be whipped and the face of the leader would be powdered white. The dishes for wine include: Turtle-like noodles and jasmine-like cheese with honey.

Seventh cup: For Emperor's wine, slow pace tune; for Prime Minister's wine, it is also slow pace tune; for officials' wine, still *Three Dais Tune*. After the dance, The announcer of Royal Band leads the girl team in. The team consist of beautiful girls over four hundred, wear flower headdress or comb hairs in a style like an immortal, and wear black dance dress; or wear scarves with rolled ends, wear brocade uniforms with four slits and embroidered with gold and red threads. All the beautiful clothes are the most in vogue at the moment to show their elegant bodies. There are four leaders for the team, they wear scarves with ends curved backward, flower hairpins, red or yellow broad sleeves clothes with bands, and hold rods with silver wrapped heads. The leaders are famous prostitutes of the capital include BrotherServant Chen(NuGe Chen),SisterBlock Zu(JieGe Zu), AccompanyServant Li(BanNu Li) and Servant Shuang(Nu Shuang), others need not to be mentioned here. Each leader is accompanied by four other team members who dress up like maids of an immortal with fairy clothes and flowers in their hands, they step forward under the drumbeats in lines(e.g., for *'Picking Up Lotus Tune'*, they would line up in front of the hall to imitate lotus and the winding balustrades when one is appreciating lotus at the side of a pond). Like the little dancers, the girl teams also come forward to the front of the hall to report their names of the teams. The announcer of Royal Band delivers greeting words of the girl teams, the leaders chant their psalms while dancing. Royal Band begin to play *'Picking Up Lotus'* tune, at the end of the music, the girl teams begin to dance while chanting. At the end of singing, the girls come forward to deliver greeting words, then girls come forward to recite greeting words and librettos of plays and lead the team onto stage, the play has two segments. At the end of the play, the announcer delivers greeting words of the team again, leads the team down from the stage. The team sing again and come down the stage in music. In comparison with little dancers, the content of the show of the girl team is increased significantly. The dishes for wine include: Roasted mutton steaks, sesame pancake and roasted sausage.

Eighth cup: For Emperor's wine, a solo singer sings 'Ta Ge'(Step on Song); for prime Minister's wine, slow pace tune; for officials, *'Three Dais Tune'*, chorus ' *Dancing on Tiptoe'*(Po Wu Xuan). The dishes for wine include: wheat flour paste cooked in shark form; steamed buns and chitterlings soup.

Ninth cup: for Emperor's wine, slow pace tune; for Prime Minister's wine, slow pace tune; for officials,*'Three Dais Tune'* as before. The right and left companies of Royal Guards wrestle with each other. The dishes for wine include: Cooked rice in soup, assorted cold dishes. Then Emperor leaves the hall and the party comes to an end.

All the cups in the party have a handle like a cup. All the wine cups in the hall are made of pure gold, all the wine cups in the corridors are made of pure silver. Other utensils are made from gold, silver, lacquerwares etc.

At the end of the party, the officials leave the palace with flowers on their heads, their attendants also wear flowers on their heads and would be given stipends by government for the activity. The girl team leave from Right Side Gate, the young men of the rich families come forward to offer various treasures to them, the girls ride on fine horses to go back. Some of the girls wear corolla, some of them wear man's clothes, they gallop through Royal Street to compete for their elegance and beauty, a lot of pedestrians stand along the street forming a wall and obstructing the way. At the end of the party holding in the auditorium of State Council, one would see same scene.

Beginning of Winter

Beginning of Winter arrives in the month. Five days before the date, West Royal Garden transport winter vegetables to Royal Palace. The capital is in cold place. There is no fresh vegetable in winter. From Royal Palace to ordinary people, they have to store winter vegetables for whole winter, thus carts for transporting vegetables to the capital would obstruct roads. Seasonable materials include: Fermented soy bean with ginger, sliced meat, mixed blood and flour cake, hard pear, sliced internal organs of pig or sheep, orange, crabs.

Volume Ten

<hr>

Winter Solstice

Winter solstice arrives in November. People of the capital pay high attention to the festival, even the poorest people would use their savings or borrowed money to change to new clothes, buy foods to pay tributes to their ancestors. The government allows people to bet, people begin to celebrate forthcoming New Year, the celebration is same as for January First.

Training of Horses, Carriages And Elephants in Advance For Grand Ceremony

For grand ceremony, the training of horses, carriages and elephants start two months early. The training takes a round trip from Declare Kindness Building to South Fragrance Gate everyday. There are five carriages to substitute for five carriages(Jade, Gold, Elephant Tusk, Leather and Wood carriages)of Emperor. There are two flags, one drum for every carriage, the carriage is pulled by four horses.The guards of the carriage all wear violet uniforms and hats. Several people are whipping in front of the carriages to clear the way. There are seven elephants, dozens of red flags, a dozens of bronze gongs and drums ahead. Strike gongs twice first, then beat drums thrice. All the people holding the flags wear violet uniforms and hats. There is man each riding on one elephant, he is sitting on the neck of the elephant(wear scarf with crossed ends and violet uniforms), holding a bronze pickaxe with sharp end, if the elephant does not act itself, the man would prick the elephant with the pickaxe. When elephants come to the front of Declare Kindness Building, the trainers would walk the elephants several rounds in empty place in the front of the building, then line them up in a column, tell them to kneel down to north direction, the elephants would respond to the order. The relatives of Emperor and the noble would call the elephants to show in front of their mansions, they would award silvers and bolts of silk to the team, the elephants really don't have free time. Visitors would come to Royal Street to watch the training of carriages and elephants like hills and oceans of people. Peddlers would sell clay, engraved wood and flour elephant figurines, the visitors would buy them and give other people as a gift when they return to their homes.

Emperor Sleep in Grand Celebration Hall

Three days before Winter Solstice, Emperor would go and stay in Grand Celebration Hall. There is a wide space in front of the hall, tens of thousands people could stand there without any problem. All the guards of honor and his procession could stand in there with plenty room left. There are two buildings standing at the sides of the hall across each other, they are called Bell and Drum Towers, people of Administration Hall Office would stay in the towers to check hourglass to report time. Every two hours and every quarter the people on duty would report time, then a man with green uniform would report time to the person on duty of the palace with his official tablet. For quarter he would report at which quarter of which time(For example five Geng third quarter, that means 3:45 am); for every hour, he would report at which hour.

Prime Minister and other officials all wear their corresponding uniforms and hats. Prime Minister and princes have mink skin on their hats as ornament, their hats have nine ridges, ministers have seven ridges, others would have six to two ridges, depending upon his rank. Imperial Censors and Supervisors have Xie Zhi(a fabulous animal reputed to be able to distinguish between good and evil) horns on their hats. For so-called ridge, it means the gold or bronze leaf ornament hanging on the frontal beam of the hat. All officials wear deep-red uniforms with black laces, a collar with round at upper part and square at lower part and shirt, jades and boots with a head looks like cloud at front, take official tablets corresponding to their ranks. Other staffs wear Jie Zhi (A long scarf which could wrap a head completely) and red uniforms according to their rank levels. Only staffs of Imperial Censorate and Supervision wear a collar with round at upper part and square at lower part. The people on duty will have different plates to show where they could go and be on duty. For guards staying within the hall, they have yellow square plate, other people will have yellow long plate or red square or long plate to show where they could go and be on duty.

The carriages and guards of honor and flags include: Imperial banners, dragon flags, wind flags, southward pointing cart, wooden, leather, elephant tusk, gold and jade decorated carriages(One could find the patterns and forms in the book of Rituals, thus it would not go further in detail here). They line up within the hall, in front of the hall and Royal Street. Royal Guards are in full gear, and tens thousands cavalrymen are riding on fine horses to guard Royal Palace around.

In the night, besides Guards of Honor and Internal Security Personnel, there are soldiers with loose uniforms and small caps with golden laces and black rods with silver wrapped head within the hall, they are called 'Shouting and Exploring Soldiers', a dozen of the soldiers form a team, there are a dozen teams. One leader would shout:"Right?" Others would shout:"Yes." The leader:"Who is it?" Others:"Commander Return Gao(Qiu Gao)." They would shout continuously and alternately, some would imitate the calling of a rooster.

There is a guard line outside of Declare Kindness Building, the soldiers on guard are called 'Gallant Soldiers'(Wei Yan Bing Shi). There are more than two hundred decorated drums with the soldiers, same number of horns are kept by the soldiers. The horns have tassels like ornaments hanging down. The soldiers wear small hat with embroidered yellow head bands, yellow embroidered loose uniforms with blue tight shirts. They would beat drums at Ri Bu(three to five o'clock in afternoon) and Three Geng(twenty three hours to one hour). Before the drums, they would blow the horns first, which means they would cordon off the area. Before the announce, they would blow horn first, at the end of horn blowing, an officer would hold a long and soft rattan with red horsetails, the drum beaters would follow his command by watching the higher or lower position of his rattan to beat the drums.

Procession of Emperor

In Five Geng, the official in charge of ritual procession with his official tablet report to Emperor everything is ready. The cavalrymen etc. of the procession have already moved from Three Geng. Seven elephants are leading in the procession with embroidered colorful brocade on their bodies, golden lotus seats are set up on their backs, golden bridles are put on their heads, the trainers are sitting on their necks with brocade uniforms. Next in line are big flags, big fans, painted halberds and long spears held by soldiers. The soldiers wear colorful armors with colorful head bands, some wear black scarves with round top, some wear helmets of leather, some wear baling bucket like helmets of scarf, some wear colorful embroidered brocade uniforms, some wear blue or black shoes, some wear trousers of pure blue or black, some wear scarves with crossed ends, some take ropes of brocade and wrap the ropes around their bodies like snake, dozens of them raise big flags while singing, some hold big axes in hand with swords hanging in waist, some hold shields, some hold rods, some hold long rods with leopard tails hanging at the top ends, some hold short rods. The spears and halberds are festooned with colorful tassels; the big flags and fans are painted with dragons, tigers, clouds or mountains and rivers. There is a flag about 15 meters high, the flag is called 'Next To Dragon Flag'. Before Emperor goes to Imperial Ancestor Temple and Blue Temples, more than a hundred people will go there in advance to erect a flag pole and flag in flag hole with rope in front of the temple.

Thousands more wear scarves with crossed ends, sword at waist, and boots. Other staffs of various departments all wear red clothes. The personal guards, attendants and retinues all wear hats, head bands, red brocade uniforms or red brocade uniforms with embroidered lion patterns. The attendants who carry personal articles of Emperor all would wear scarves with bead knot at the top, violet clothes with embroidered flowers in various colors, golden waist bands, and silk shoes. The soldiers of Natural Valor would wear red bamboo hats painted with golden patterns, red uniforms with embroidered flowers. Other soldiers and officers with weapons wear small hats, violet uniforms with embroidered flowers, they ride on horses to lead the procession. Thousands of horses come out of Declare Kindness Building and go to Imperial Ancestors Temple.

Emperor's Sleep in Imperial Ancestors Temple and Calling out Tablets of Ancestors

Emperor takes Jade Carriage, his clothes look like the ones in painting in charge of constellations, his crown is decorated with pearl strings from cold north of the country, he wears deep red robe, holds the Prime Tablet. The Jade Carriage's roof is composed of carved gold lotus leaves, the columns and balustrades are with engraved flowers, dragons and phoenixes. The carriage is pulled by four horses, immediately followed by flags with embroidered suns and moons and dragons. There is a royal seat in the carriage, only two personal attendants staying in the carriage, one is standing at the side to be ready to answer questions of Emperor, he is called 'Control Peace'(Zhi Sui). The guards protecting the carriage wear black scarves without ends, colorful yellow loose uniforms, blue tight shirts, blue trousers with brocade ropes. Four people hold signs for forbidding pass behind the carriage. In front of the carriage, two people with official uniforms hold their official tablets, face the carriage and walk backwards.

In the night Emperor stay in Imperial Ancestors Temple, his guards just act like the ones in Grand Celebration Hall. At Three Geng(11pm-1am), Emperor begins to take part in praying, all the attendants are relatives of Emperor. Royal Band play music, Emperor stands at the southeast corner facing westward in the hall, there is a red plank with golden characters 'Emperor's Position'. Then Emperor would take the tablets of his ancestors and go out of the hall, the officials also would cordon off the areas. Emperor goes to rooms with tablets of Empresses to pay his tributes, then the cavalrymen, guards of honor, carriages would come out Imperial Ancestors Temple and go out of South Fragrance Gate.

Emperor Goes to Blue Hall

Emperor goes to Blue Hall in Jade Carriage. For Blue Call, in past it was just a fasting place enclosed by blue screen with painted bricks and balustrade patterns temporarily to form towers, palaces and buildings. In the period of 1111 to 1125 AD, Great Ancestor Emperor Hui orders to build the hall with bricks and woods. Elite cavalrymen are guarding at the perimeter of the place. All soldiers wear violet scarves and red uniforms without armors, there are more than a thousand soldiers guarding the place, there are a dozen musicians in the team. Patrol commander leads the team, they patrol the place all the night. In the night, the drums, and the security follow the practice of Grand Celebration Hall as before.

Emperor Goes to Pray Temple at South of The Capital

At three Geng, Emperor goes to Pray Temple at south of the capital. There are three short walls around the pray temple. Emperor leaves Blue Hall, goes southward for about 500 meters to come to the pray temple. Emperor goes in through east gate of first wall, enters the side of second wall, there is a screen facing southward within the second wall, it is called 'Big Screen'. Emperor changes his clothes for pray in the screen: a crown with twenty four tassels, blue robe with embroidered dragons with shirts, red shoes and white jade pendant at waist. Emperor goes to the front of the round high place supported by two attendants. At the foot of the high pray place there is another little screen, there is a seat for Emperor in the screen.

The pray place is about three layers with seventy two steps, the perimeter of the place is about 10 meters. There are four paths to the place: at the south it is called Wu Steps, at the east it is called Mao Steps, at the west it is called You Steps and at the north it is called Zi Steps(Wu, Mao, You and Zi are twelve numbers for earth in calendar of China still in use). There are two yellow quilts with tablets. The one in the north facing south is called Great Heaven Emperor, the one in southeast is called Great First Ancestor Emperor(The tablet for the first emperor of the dynasty). There are only two short tables with tributes on the tables. There are a dozen of Taoist monks in the place who are chanting for pray, with two bells and chimes and other music instruments, and three to five performers for each kind of instruments.

There are music instrument stands in front of the place: In the front row are jade chimes and iron chimes. They look just like ordinary ones except to large sizes. The iron chimes are thinner than ordinary ones, there are two columns in the stand, and tassels at the corners of the stand. The jade chimes look like curved rule, the curved places are their pointed ends, they are also hung in a stand in two columns.

Next line are big drums in three or five, they are bound with wooden poles and are hung in stands. There are big bells, the bells are called Prosperous Bells(Jin Zhong), there are drums called Jie Drum(A kind of ancient drums). There are qins(A seven string plucked instruments) but bigger than usual ones; there are Zheng (A plucked instruments with twenty five strings like harp) but larger than usual ones; there are flutes but bigger than usual ones; there are Xuns(egg-shaped holed wind instruments) and vertical flutes.

There are singers who sing loudly and clearly, which is much better than the ones sang by people in Zheng and Wei states in Warring Periods(475-221 BC). There are two poles in front of the stands, the performers all wear long scarves like Jie Zhe (Long scarves form a pattern like a cage in one's head), red loose clothes and silk waist bands. Two dancers wear violet hats, black clothes, red skirts and black leather shoes.

At the beginning there is a scholarly dance, the dancer would hold a violet bag with a flute, the flute had ribbon bands. Then soldierly dance, the dancer hold a little spear in one hand and a small shield in the other. The number of dancers are more in soldiers dance than the scholarly dance, they strike bronze cymbals and rattle rings, some are striking an instrument like a bronze stove, some two are carrying a bronze vat and beating it on ground. Some dancers were piercing with spear and parrying with shield as if they were flying above clouds or parting with each other etc. Then Royal Music begins to play, first begin to strike Chu(An ancient music instrument looks like a square kettle with painted mountains and rivers at the surface), they strike Chu for nine times at the inside and outside. At the end of Chu, they would strike Yu(Yu, a music instrument looks like a crouching tiger with saw teeth like patterns on its back), near the end of the play, the Yu will be stricken with bamboo slices.

The ritual hosting officer asks Emperor to climb to the temple. The ushers leads Emperor to the front of the high round pray hill, only hosting officer and his attendants could climb the steps with Emperor. The officer first bow to the tablet at north side, kowtow, then put wine in front of the tablet, his attendant bow to the tablet at east side, put wine in front of the tablet, kowtow twice. Then Emperor climbs the steps, Royal Band stop play, the performers at the pray place begin to perform climbing music; Emperor climbs down the place, Royal Band begin to play again, soldierly dance begin to play again, Emperor goes back to Little Screen again. Similar rituals are performed for second and third pray. At that time Prince Yan and Prince Yue led the prays. Emperor climbs the pray place for second time, music plays in same fashion as before, he kowtows to the tablets and pour wines, an officer in charge of imperial decrees begin to announce imperial decree while kneeling down on ground, his two attendants are holding the decree for him. Emperor goes down to Little Screen again. Second and Third Prays repeat again like before. Emperor climbs the pray place again, dedicate wine in jade cups, drinks wine. Second and Third Prays repeat again like before and climb down the pray place. Emperor stands in front of Little Screen, the tributes, silk money and jade booklets all are taken down from the pray place from You steps. Outside of the south wall, one hundred twenty meters away from the pray place, there is a burning stove about 3 meters high, all things from the pray place are burnt in the stove. One is counting and another one is burning in the stove. There are twelve shrines along the curved walls and the steps to the pray place in the three walls, they are used to pray to twelve gods, several hundred stars are dedicated with tributes outside of the innermost wall. The hosting officer and other attendants are already standing facing northward according to their ranks. The musics from the pray place have already stopped, the blowing music has not started yet, hundred thousands people stand quietly in the pray place and around, they could only hear the clinking sound of jade pendants on their clothes in wind, one hosting officer shouts loudly:"Bow first!" All people begin to bow, then the grand pray comes to an end.

Back to Palace From Grand Pray

Emperor returns to Big Screen from Small Screen, about two hundred attendants with big rod candles form a wall around the screen. Emperor enters the screen, changes his clothes to usual ones, climb on a big palanquin (As big as Jade Carriage without wheels and with yellow tassels hanging at four corners), the bearers of the palanquin wear same clothes as other guards who are protecting the carriage and palanquin. As soon as Emperor gets into the palanquin, Royal Band who has already stood at the outer wall from east to west begin to play music, a soldier with armors play a dance with a tune of *Po*(Break), at the end of the dance, the leader of Royal Band delivers psalm, Music Band plays again, other musicians in the army joins to play, the sound of music is piercing into sky and shattering the ground.

When they return to Blue Hall, the day is not break yet, officials with uniforms enter the hall to congratulate Emperor for successful end of Grand Pray. Emperor rewards the officials with tea and wine, then Emperor returns to his palace with guards of honor, cavalrymen and Music Band through South Fragrance Gate. Along dozens kilometers Royal Street, tents are set up by officials and the rich and powerful families to greet the procession. The beautiful tents are filled along the street without a bit empty space.

Amnesty

Emperor goes to Declare Kindness Building. There are several big flags in front of the building. The tall one is as high as the building, it is called 'Sky Covers Flag'(Gai Tian Qi). The flag stands at the center of Royal Street motionlessly. The shorter one comes with the procession of Emperor, it is called 'Yellow Dragon Next'(Ci Huang Long). Blue Hall and Imperial Ancestors Temple also erect flags in front of them, ordinary people also call them 'Sky Cover Flag'. There are also stands for music instruments. Soon the band begins to play music and strike clappers for announcing time in night. Then a pole is erected, the pole is dozen meters high. There is a big wooden plate at the top of the pole, there is a gold chicken in the plate, the chicken holds a red banner in its mouth, the banner is with characters of 'Long Live Emperor', there are four colorful bands hanging down from the bottom of the plate. There are four men climbing to get the red banners, the winner get the red banner of Gold Chicken, the winner kowtows to Emperor for his reward. There is a red rope hanging down from the top of the building to the tent at the foot of the building, a golden phoenix holds amnesty paper, the leader at the tent announces the amnesty. The prisoners are kept in front of the tents by Municipal Government of Capital and High Court, all the prisoners wear red clothes with yellow patches, the prisoner guards all wear head flowers and clean clothes. Upon hearing the drumbeat, they release the prisoners, all the prisoners kowtow to Emperor, then they left as ordinary people as they get their amnesty. At the foot of the building, Royal Band begin to play music, play, dancing, the royal guard play ghosts and immortals, cut with real knives, Emperor holds a party for the officials at the upper floor of the building. The guards begin to take back their horses and return to their barracks. At breakfast in next morning, the ceremony of amnesty comes to an end.

Emperor Returns to His Palace, at Certain Auspicious Dates Emperor Goes to Various Temple To Express His Thanks

Emperor returns to his palace. He would go to West and East Ancestors Temple to express his thanks to his ancestors. The activity lasts for three days. At the end of the third day, he would visit the one of palaces of his concubines or one of the mansions of his ministers. In the month, businessmen sell glutinous rice cakes, quails, rabbits etc.

December

Businessmen begin to sell artificial flowers, hotbed chives, lettuce, tender leaves of orchid, peppermints, walnut, and maltose from Ze Prefecture. In December 8th, groups of monks in three to five people go to street to chant sutras, they would hold a silver gilded bronze basin or other basin in good quality, put a wooden statute of Buddha within the basin bathed in scented water, bath the statute with the water using a willow branch, beg along households in street or alley. Temples of the capital hold December 8th porridge donation, send porridge to their disciples, the porridge is called December 8th porridge(The practice is still in practice till now). In the day people of the capital would prepare porridge with various ingredients. In the date temples would send oil and wheat flour to their disciples plus the alms register, the temple would raise money for Lantern Festival. People in the capital exchange gifts with each other.

In the month,Treasured Register Temple at Revere Dragon Gate would hold lantern festivals in advance. The people are bustling around. December 24th, it is little New Year, people of the capital invites monks to recite sutras, prepare wine and other tributes to send immortals to report back to Heaven, burn paper money, attach the god of kitchen at the side of the kitchen, spread dregs of wine at the door of the kitchen stove, it is called 'Drunk Commander'(Zui Si Ming). In the night, people would leave a lighted lamp under bed, it is called 'Light Loss'(Zhao Xu Hao).

In the month no other festivals, but the rich would hold a party as long as it is snowing, they would make snow lion, snow lamp and mouth, meet their old and new friends. As New Year comes near, businessmen begin to sell paintings of God of Door, peach plank and peach wood charms to fight against ghosts, paintings of fortune of good(It is called

Fortune of God on Back of A Donkey as it is sold in that fashion) and Generals and New Year's couplets. Businessmen sell dried eggplant, purslane, and sticky maltose for usage in New Year's Eve. For poor people they would dress up like women, immortals and ghosts, strike gongs and beat drums to drive away ghosts to beg along streets and alleys, it is called 'Beat Night Ghost'(Da Ye Hu), it is a way to drive a way ghost.

New Year's Eve

In the day of New Year's Eve, the palace would hold a grand ritual Da Nuo Yi(To drive ghosts away). All the people on duty would wear masks and colorful clothes, hold golden spears and dragon flags. The leader of Royal Band FirstScene Meng is tall and sturdy, he wears gold gilt bronze armors to play as a general. There are two people act as Towering Generals to protect the palace as God of Gate. The leader of Royal Band 'Coal at South Bank' would act as an ugly official working in Hell. Some people would act as the sister of Xun Zhong(An immortal good at catching ghosts), gods of earth, gods of kitchen stove etc., more than a thousand of people dress up, they would drive ghosts away from the palace till the outside of South Fragrance Gate. They would turn outside of South Fragrance Gate, it is called 'Bury Ghosts'. In the night, the palace would set off firecrackers all the night, people could hear the sound from faraway places. Ordinary people would sit around a stove, stay awake for all the night, it is called 'Shou Sui'(Guard Against Sui - a ghost who incurs damage to people, till the moment in some places people are still doing same thing).

I only witnessed the practice of Grand Ceremonies, but I did not take part in real activities. Thus I might miss some crucial parts, I would be more than glad if you could give correct answers.

Did you love *Dreamlike Recording of East Capital*? Then you should read *Empress Wu Zetian 1*[1] by Nangong Bo!

[2]

In the great dynasties of China there are many tales of corruption, espionage, and intrigue, but perhaps no tale is more intriguing than the rise of China's first and only female Emperor, Wu Zetian (624-705).

In the hierarchies of Imperial China, there are many who call themselves empress, and there are many who held sway over their weak-minded emperor husbands, but only Wu Zetian reached the pinnacle when at the age of 65 she usurped her son and became the undisputed Empress of Tang Dynasty China.

Empress Wu Zetian was the only female emperor in Chinese history, honored as the Holy and Divine Emperor of Wu Zhou. Her

---

1. https://books2read.com/u/mB8Pyy

2. https://books2read.com/u/mB8Pyy

original name was Wu Mei Niang, and she changed her name to Wu Zhao after ascending the throne.

She entered the palace as a concubine of Emperor Taizong of Tang, but she had a close relationship with the future Emperor Gaozong, Li Chih. After Emperor Taizong's death, she entered the Gan Ye Temple and became a nun. The power struggle in the harem brought her back to the palace, where she successfully eliminated her rivals and was made Empress in 655. She participated in politics and was known as the "Two Saints" along with Emperor Gaozong. After Emperor Gaozong's death, she controlled the government. In 690, she ascended to the throne and proclaimed herself the Holy Emperor, changing Luoyang to the Divine Capital and the country's name to Zhou. This period is known as the Southern Zhou or Wu Zhou in history.

This book starts its plot from the time when Wu Zetian was constrained in Gan Ye Temple after the former Emperor (Taizong) was deceased and how the new Emperor (Gaozong) brought her to the court again. Later, she gradually realized her dream of becoming the most powerful woman in the palace through bloody struggles and bold strategies.

She had outstanding abilities in governing the country, but in the power struggle within the palace, she showed an extremely cruelty, being ruthless and killing innocent people. In order to clear obstacles and eliminate political enemies in the struggle for imperial power, she carried out bloody killings time and time again, not even sparing her own descendants.